# THE ULTIMATE GUIDE TO COOKING RICE

## THE INDIAN WAY

**Prasenjeet Kumar**

**Copyright Prasenjeet Kumar 2015**

All rights reserved. No part of this book may be reproduced, stored in a retrieval system, or transmitted, in any form or by any means, electronic, mechanical, photocopying, recording or otherwise, without the prior permission of the copyright owner, except in the case of brief quotations embodied in critical articles or reviews.

To economise on costs, this book contains no photographs. However, if you wish to have a look at how the dishes should actually look like, you could either refer to the e-Book version (which you can download for FREE if you purchase this Book under the Kindle Matchbook Programme) or to the Author's website www.cookinginajiffy.com.

**Your FREE Gift**

As a way of saying thanks for your purchase, I'm offering an e-book FREE as a gift.

Cooking home-made meals can do wonders for your health and well-being. But a lot of times, a hectic work schedule does not let couples create meals from scratch at home. I get a lot of questions from readers who are willing to cook at home but do not find the necessary time and energy to do so.

In this PDF (which is a 154-page or 22,000 word document), I share the tips and techniques that anyone can use to create a complete breakfast, lunch or dinner from scratch in less than 30 minutes.

You can download this free e-book by going here:

http://eepurl.com/SVaoz

## Disclaimers

Although the Author has made every effort to ensure that the information in this book was correct at the time of publication, the Author does not assume and hereby disclaims any liability to any party for any loss, damage, or disruption caused by errors or omissions, whether such errors or omissions result from negligence, accident, or any other cause.

This book is not intended as a substitute for the medical advice of physicians. The reader should regularly consult a physician in matters relating to his/her health and particularly with respect to any symptoms that may require diagnosis or medical attention.

This book also assumes that the reader does not suffer from any food allergies or related medical conditions. Readers suffering from food allergies are requested to skip the recipes that contains ingredients which trigger adverse reactions in that reader or in his/her family and friends.

***The spellings used in this book are British, which may look strange to my American friends, but NOT to those living in Australia, Canada, India, Ireland and of course the United Kingdom. This means that color is written as colour and so on. I hope that is NOT too confusing!***

*"Rice is a beautiful food. It is beautiful when it grows, precision rows of sparkling green stalks shooting up to reach the hot summer sun. It is beautiful when harvested, autumn gold sheaves piled on diked, patchwork paddies. It is beautiful when, once threshed, it enters granary bins like a (flood) of tiny seed-pearls. It is beautiful when cooked by a practiced hand, pure white and sweetly fragrant."*

**Shizuo Tsuji**

# Table of Contents

I: Rice-My Personal Story 1

II: Rice—Why Bother? 5

III: Rice in India 13

Chapter 1: Just Rice 19

    Rice Boiled 20
    Curd Rice 24
    Lemon rice 26
    Tamarind rice 28
    Tomato rice 30
    Onion Rice 32
    *Jeera Pulao* (Cumin Rice) 34
    Saffron *pulao* (Saffron rice dish) 38

Chapter 2: Rice Cooked with Lentils 43

    *Khichdi* (Mixture of Rice, Lentil and Veggies Dish) 43

*Chana Dal Khichdi* (Rice dish cooked with split chick pea) 48

Light *Khichdi* 52

*Pongal* 55

*Bisi Belle Bhath* 58

Chapter 3: Rice Cooked with Veggies 63

*Mattar Pulao* (Peas Rice) 63

Dry Fruits *Pulao* 68

Mixed Vegetable Cheese *Biryani* 73

*Navratna Pulao* (Nine Jewels Rice dish) 79

Stir Fried Rice 85

Chapter 4: Rice Cooked with Meats 89

Prawn Stir Fried Rice 89

Chicken *Biryani* 92

Hyderabadi Chicken *Biryani* 101

Chicken *Kofta* (Mince ball) *Biryani* 105

Mutton *Biryani* 111

Chapter 5: Rice as Snacks and Accompaniments 119

*Chiura* or *Poha* Fry (Savoury Rice Flakes) 119

*Poha* (Cooked Rice Flakes) 122

*Idlis* (Steamed rice and lentil cakes) 124

*Dosa* 126

*Baigun Bhaja* (Aubergine fries) 129

Chapter 6: Rice as Desserts 131

*Chawal Ka Kheer* (Rice Pudding) 131

*Natun Gud Ka Kheer* (Rice Pudding with Palm Jaggery) 133

*Phirni* (Ground Rice Custard) 135

Sweet Rice With Mango 137

Sweet *Pongal* 139

*Sakkarai Pongal* (Sweet rice-lentil dessert with milk) 142

Sweet *Poha Kheer* (Rice Flakes Pudding) 146

Appendix: An Introduction to the Common Indian Spices 147

A Big Thank You! 153

Excerpt from Home Style Indian Cooking In A Jiffy 155

Acknowledgement 169

Other Books By The Author 171

Books by the Author in Other Genres 181

Connect With The Author 189

About The Author 191

Index 193

# I

## Rice-My Personal Story

Whenever the word 'rice' is mentioned, it invokes all kinds of deep emotions within me.

My mom and dad used to make fun of me when I was a little boy. This is because I needed rice for lunch and dinner and would just not eat anything if it wasn't served with rice.

You would have guessed by now that I am from a different planet. A planet called 'India' which is located in a solar system called 'Asia'.

When I was 3 years old, my mom and dad took me to another planet known as the United States of America, more specifically to a country inside that planet known as Los Angeles where my uncle lived.

The strangest thing I found about this planet was that there was no rice. My uncle served soups, sausages, pizzas, burgers and spaghetti but no rice!

"Is there no food to eat?" I queried after seeing an apparently "food-laden" table, that left my uncle shell- shocked and my parents not knowing where to look.

"What a Mr. Rice Eater!" I was referred to as by that name.

Today, I am no longer that fussy. I can eat anything for lunch or dinner and am fine with anything and everything. Be it soups, sandwiches, pizzas, pastas or rice! May be I have been corrupted by adulthood, changes in lifestyle, living and studying for four years in a planet called England. However, rice continues to have a special place in my heart.

Rice tastes really well with curries especially with my home made variation of Butter Chicken or British Chicken Tikka Masala. The Indian Basmati rice is my favourite and something I eat at my home by default. But I also love the Thai variety known as 'Jasmine rice' which has a very sweet fragrance that tastes absolutely fabulous with the Thai Green or Red or Penang curry.

This is not to say that I don't like bread. While living in Europe for nearly four years, I had to develop a taste for all kinds of bread. Every bread has its own taste, texture and hardness and I love that. But today

I am going to talk about only rice, my home and comfort food.

I find rice very filling that also gives me good sleep. By the way, medical research has established that rice boosts your serotonin levels making you happy and helping you sleep better. So I am not just imagining things my way!

I am also an absolute defender of rice against 'Western onslaught' (forgive me for using that term) of claims that rice leads to obesity, or to increased body fat. Mind you I love rice, yet have a flat belly. That is because I regulate my diet and exercise regularly.

In this background, I present to you over the next chapters the nutritional benefits of having rice and the richness of the cultural tradition associated with rice in India. After that you shall be free to savour over thirty really mouth-watering my Home Style rice recipes constituting main dishes, side dishes, snacks and even desserts.

Bon appetit then!

Prasenjeet

## II

### Rice—Why Bother?

*"A diet that consists predominantly of rice leads to the use of opium, just as a diet that consists predominantly of potatoes leads to the use of liquor."*

**Friedrich Nietzsche**

*"Only rice likes to be drowned."*

**Charles de Leusse**

Doesn't eating rice make you pot-bellied, like those Chinese "Laughing Buddha" figurines?

Okay. Let's disregard that as one of the old-wives' tales.

Because if you look at people who live in villages in any part of Asia: India, China, Thailand, Vietnam, Japan, Cambodia, etc., where rice is the staple food, you will hardly find anyone who is fat or pot-bellied.

But speaking scientifically, isn't rice so full of useless starch, with less than 1% fat and really negligible amounts of protein?

Ahhhh......yes.

So who really needs rice?

How about 70% of the world?

Or, almost any part of the world which is wet and humid and NOT colder than 21 degree Celsius (70 degree F)?

Including USA and northern Canada?

Now we are talking.

## The medicinal and nutritional properties of rice

Rice is "popular" because it is one of the easiest foods to digest. Being totally gluten free, it is the best food for infants when they have to be weaned. For young adults and old people too, who may have wheat allergies or even celiac disease, eating rice would be what every sensible doctor would prescribe.

For the same reason, rice is great for relieving digestive disorders like diarrhoea, dysentery, colitis and even morning sickness.

In many traditional remedies, rice powder is used as a soothing agent in skin infections or inflammations for diseases ranging from chicken-pox and measles to prickly heat and simple burns.

Rice is high in complex carbohydrates, contains almost no fat, is cholesterol free, and is low in sodium. It is a fair source of protein containing all eight essential amino acids. It is low in the amino acid lysine, which is found in beans and lentils, making the classic combination of rice and beans, popularly known as complementary proteins, a particularly healthy dish.

The soluble fibre in brown rice helps lower the levels of 'bad' LDL cholesterol in the blood. The fibre also helps in increasing the digestion time of this carbohydrate, as compared to other processed grains. This means that it has a lower glycaemic index (GI) compared to other grains that helps release sugar into the blood stream in a very slow and controlled manner.

Half a cup of cooked brown rice typically provides 89 calories; 0 grams fat, including saturated fat or trans-fat, 0 milligrams sodium, 45 grams total carbohydrate (15% Daily Value), 0 grams sugar, 3 grams of protein, and some vitamins like B1 or thiamine (0.34 mg), riboflavin (0.05 mg), and niacin (4.7 mg).

## A little history would now be in order

Experts are almost unanimous that while rice has grown in India from time immemorial, it was taken to Greece by Alexander the Great around 327 B.C.

Eastwards, it probably travelled with Buddhist monks (and intrepid South Indian traders) to China, Korea, Japan, Thailand, Indonesia and all other countries of South-East Asia, where in any case some other varieties of rice were already growing in the wild.

Arab travellers introduced rice to Egypt, Morocco and Spain. Persian speaking tribes invading India took it to Persia, Turkey and Central Asia. Portugal and Netherlands took rice to their colonies in West Africa. And the Spaniards introduced rice to the Americas through the 'Columbian Exchange' of natural resources.

## Some nuggets about rice production

Believe it or not, but an Australian Government Report claimed that almost 140,000 wild and cultivated rice varieties have been identified so far. As per World Encyclopaedia, farmers even today cultivate 7000 to 8000 varieties of rice.

However, the most popular world cuisines use just three prominent varieties of rice: *Indica* the long-grained aromatic variety that is grown in India as Basmati rice; *Japonica* which is the shorter and sticky variety that is popular in Japan for sushi and in Mediterranean countries for dishes such as risotto and paella; and *Javanica* which is medium grained, falls somewhat in between *Indica* and *Japonica* in terms of stickiness, and is popular in South-East Asia and China.

Paddies, which literally mean puddles of water, depict a very interesting agricultural practice. Despite seemingly standing in water, they actually conserve water, as opposed to all other forms of farming that require constant irrigation. When located on hilly slopes, as "terrace farms", they look so picturesque and picture postcard perfect that they can take literally your breath away.

These plants are so tough that they adapt even to rising flood waters. For example, some varieties in Bangladesh bear their grain above the surface of the water, sometimes to depths of even five meters! A pastor of Nagaland state in India recently received a Guinness World Record certificate for discovering a 2.55 meter (8.5 feet) tall rice plant. The certificate acknowledges that the rice plant, which the pastor found in October 1998 in the state´s Chumukedi area "had 175 stalks and 510 grains in each ear" making it the tallest paddy species found so far in the world.

In 2003, to make sure that the giant rice plant was not a freak of nature, the pastor Melhite sowed the grains taken from the original plant and planted them in his compound. The experiment produced similar results with the new paddy plants measuring

9 feet, having 240 stalks and 460 grains in each ear with each plant yielding 1.18 kg grains average.

Transplanting paddy is a very interesting agricultural practice. One- to six-week-old seedlings are transplanted to basically give them a head start over other competing weeds. Transplanting paddy also lets the farmer adjust the planting calendar to accommodate his labour, water, and other requirements. But still, for most small holdings, cultivating paddy remains a back-breaking work.

In USA too, wealthy rice plantations before the Civil War used to have hundreds of slaves. The 1849 gold rush brought many immigrants to California, including an estimated 40,000 Chinese, whose staple food was rice. Rice production then became a necessity.

But today technology has reduced the inherent drudgery involved in rice cultivation. American mega-farms now use laser technology to level field and to remove broken grains from the milled rice. Fields are seeded by airplanes, and harvested by a single combine operator.

World rice production in 2014-15, according to the USDA, is estimated to exceed 475 million metric tonnes. USA grows almost 7 million tonnes which is surprisingly as much as what Japan grows and slightly more than what Pakistan grows.

U.S. in fact is the world's 12th largest exporter of rice. Arkansas, northern California and Texas are leading growers. California alone exports some 400,000 tons of rice to all over the world.

And this is when legend has it that rice reached the USA by accident in 1685, when a storm-damaged ship from Madagascar took shelter in Charleston, South Carolina. The captain of the ship gifted a small bag of gold coloured rice to a local farmer.

The rest, as it is said, is History.

**The ways rice is now consumed**

Rice, of whatever kind, is not just used as a bed for curries or a wrapper for sushi. It is also being cooked with meats in *Biryanis*, with seafood in Paella, with wine in Risotto, with lentils in *Khichdi*, and with aromatic spices in *Pilaf*.

Rice flour is used in making pancakes and all kinds of snacks in India.

Rice now has entered the breakfast space with such ready to eat products as popped and puffed rice, and rice flakes.

Rice is used for such fermented drinks as *Chhang* without which no festive occasion is considered complete in Ladakh, Tibet, or Bhutan.

Rice straw is used as cattle feed, for thatching roof, and for making hats, mats, ropes, and sound absorbing straw boards.

Rice husk is used for making paper as well as briquettes to be used as fuel source.

Rice bran is used in cattle and poultry feed.

Defatted bran, which is rich in protein, is used in the preparation of biscuits and again as cattle feed.

Refined Rice bran oil is used for cooking. Rice bran wax, a by-product of rice bran oil, is used for making soaps and lubricating material.

Phew! Do we need to say anything more about the myriad ways in which the paddy plant benefits mankind?

# III

## Rice in India

The love affair that Indians have with rice is legendary. Rice has been a sacred grain, with some of the ancient Indian holy books like the Vedas simply referring to it as *annam*, meaning food.

Every religious ceremony has to involve rice. Rice is stuck on the red vermillion that is applied to your forehead as *akshat*, literally meaning something which is indestructible.

Rice is poured into the fire lit during religious ceremonies as *havis* or offering to gods.

Rice is sprinkled over guests, worshippers and the newlyweds to bless them.

Only rice can form the base (*asanam*) for placing the sacred pot (*kalasham*) upon it during religious ceremonies.

In certain parts of India, the bride and bridegroom are made to even stand on a pile of rice during the marriage ceremony. In North India, when a bride enters her husband's house, she is made to first knock over with her right foot a small metal jar full of rice to signify that with the spilled rice, she is bringing prosperity to the house.

Rice is vital in the ceremony of *Annaprashana*, a ritualised first feeding, which is conducted in the baby's sixth or seventh month of life. Mashed boiled rice or a sweet rice pudding called *kheer* is generally fed to the child accompanied with the chanting of sacred mantras.

When priests or elders bless you, they wish that your life be full of *dhan* (wealth) and *dhanya* (rice). Do you notice the similarity between the two words?

The biggest harvest festivals in India are linked to the time when rice is harvested. *Bihu* in Assam, *Pongal* in Tamil Nadu, *Onam* in Kerala and *Makar Sakranti* in North India—are all festivals where newly harvested rice is offered to the gods amidst lots of dancing and revelry that stretches over 2-3 days. In *Pongal*, the day's celebrations include an early morning ceremony of boiling rice with milk and sugar in clay pots, which is allowed to boil over, signifying prosperity.

There are also smaller festivals linked to pre-sowing, sowing, pre-transplanting, transplanting, invoking the rain gods, protecting, and pre-harvesting.

Phew! Looks like the ancient Indians had no other obsession bigger than the quality of the rice growing in their backyards!

Dr Richharia, the well-known rice scientist states that 400,000 varieties of rice existed in India during the Vedic period. He estimates that even today 200,000 varieties of rice exist in India, and has gone on to catalogue 20,000 types of rice in one state (Chattisgarh) alone.

Perennial wild rice still grows in the wetlands of Assam and in the border area with Nepal. Paddy grains found during excavation at Hastinapur (near Delhi) around 1000-750 B.C. are considered to be the oldest sample in the world.

There is hardly any type of soil in which rice cannot be grown including alkaline and acidic soils. Rice crop has also got wide physical adaptability. Therefore, it is grown from below sea-level (Kuttanad area of Kerala) up to an elevation of 2000 metres (6000 feet approximately) in the Himalayan regions of India from Jammu and Kashmir to Arunachal Pradesh.

Rice appears to have travelled to southern India after its domestication in the northern plains. It then spread to all the fertile alluvial plains watered by rivers. Some say that the word rice is derived from the Tamil word *arisi*.

However, the world recognises India for its North Indian Basmati rice which is an exceptionally aromatic, long-grain, slender, and non-glutinous grain. Translated literally from Hindi, it means "queen of scents." Scientifically speaking, this aroma is due to the presence of a chemical called 2-acetyl-1-pyrroline, which is found in basmati rice at about 90 parts per billion. That's about 12 times more than in any other type of rice, giving basmati its unique stature.

When cooked, Basmati rice swells only lengthwise, resulting in long slender grains that are very dry, light and separate. —not sticky. In India there is a saying that grains of rice should be like two brothers, close but not stuck together.

Obviously, that is possible only with Basmati and not with any of the *Japonica* or *Javanica* varieties.

Indians cook rice with anything and everything; with lentils, veggies, meat, fish, chicken and seafood. In addition, they have plain or spiced rice as a bed for curries and ground rice for making all kinds of pancakes like *appams* and *dosas*. Rice flour is also used for crisping *savouries* called *pakoras*.

Most temples serve as *prasadam* (blessings) the Indian rice pudding called *kheer* or *payasam*. And then in many Himalayan states, from Ladakh to Sikkim, fermented rice is used for making the potent brew called *chhang*.

With this short introduction, I present eight plain rice recipes, five recipes for cooking rice with lentils, five each for cooking rice with vegetables and meats, five ways to use rice in snacks and seven as desserts.

There is no Chhang recipe, sadly because that is one dish that is not made in my house!

# Chapter 1

## Just Rice

In this chapter, we will start with the basics.

First, how to make plain boiled rice that can serve as a bed for curries.

Then we will convert this to four really delicious South Indian dishes of Curd Rice, Lemon Rice, Tamarind Rice and Tomato Rice.

The North Indian variation is presented through the Onion Rice recipe.

Thereafter we graduate to making the simple pulao or Cumin Rice and then the more exotic Saffron Pulao.

Master these eight recipes and you would have captured the essence of cooking rice the Indian way.

## Rice Boiled

*Ingredients*

Rice-1 cup

Water-2 cups

Tip: Use the same cup please! Otherwise, your rice will NOT turn out to be fluffy.

Wash the rice well (*in a vessel 3-4 times, but don't rub it lest the grains break*) and let it naturally "dry", on an inclined plate, for 15-20 minutes. This helps enhance the aroma.

If you have a Rice Cooker, follow its instructions. Otherwise, I present three popular methods below to turn out a perfect plate of boiled rice.

*Method using a pressure cooker*

In a pressure cooker (3-5 litre capacity or 6-11 US pints capacity) bring the water to a boil.

Add the rice to the boiling water.

Close the lid of the pressure cooker BUT remove the weight.

When steam starts escaping from the vent (*don't worry, you will hear that typical sound*), reduce the heat to minimum. In other words, if cooking on gas, turn the knob to SIM (mer).

Wait for 10 minutes and switch off the gas. Take out the rice. Your hot fluffy rice is ready.

*Method using a thick bottomed vessel/deep pan*

In a vessel or a pan, bring the water to a boil.

Add the rice to the boiling water. Turn the heat to low and cover the vessel/deep pan with a well-fitting lid.

Cook for 15-20 minutes without stirring the rice. Switch off the heat source. Lift the lid and check whether the rice is properly cooked.

Cooked rice is always soft. To check, you have to take out a grain of rice and press it between your fingers (obviously use a spoon to take out the grain to avoid scalding your hands).

If the grain is still hard, that means it is under cooked. If it is soft, then it is cooked properly.

In case the grain is not properly cooked, you may like to add another ½ cup of water and let it cook on low heat for another 7-10 minutes.

*Traditional method (the way it is cooked in villages or dhabas even today)*

In a vessel or a pan, bring three (instead of two mentioned in the above two methods) cups of water (for one cup of rice) to a boil.

Add the rice to the boiling water. Turn the heat to medium and don't cover the vessel/deep pan, because the water will boil and spill over.

Cook for 15-20 minutes stirring the rice gently from time to time. Keep on checking whether the rice is properly cooked.

Once the rice is done, switch off the heat source. Drain all the excess water. (You can use a colander. Traditionally, the vessel will just be covered with a lid and the water poured out. This is tricky as both the vessel and the water would be very hot.)

Although the traditional method takes more time, it is believed to bring out the flavours better. Since the water used for boiling the rice is totally drained out, some dieticians claim that this method helps take out some of the starch from the rice thus shaving off some calories from this dish.

Tip: The drained out water can act as an excellent stock for soups especially when it comes out of the local red coloured rice.

*Method using a rice cooker*

Place the rice and water in the rice cooker.

Close the lid and switch on the cooker. The rice will be cooked and the rice cooker will switch off on its own.

This is the easiest and the most fool proof way of making rice.

Prep time: 20 minutes

Cooking time: 10 minutes with a pressure cooker; 15-20 minutes with a deep pan; and as indicated in the rice cooker manual

Total time: 30 minutes with a pressure cooker; 35-40 minutes with a deep pan

## Curd Rice

This is a very simple, light and delicious dish to have in hot summers. This is a perennial favourite all over Southern India, where many prefer ending their meals NOT with a dessert but with curd rice!

*Ingredients*

Cooked rice-2 cups

Yoghurt-1 cup

Clarified butter (*Ghee*)-1 tablespoon

Black Mustard-1/2 teaspoon

Ginger-1/2 inch piece chopped up finely

Curry leaves-a few

Roasted *Chana dal* (split chick peas)-1/2 teaspoon

Salt to taste

*Optional*: You can also add finely sliced carrots and deseeded, chopped green chillies for flavour if you so desire.

*Method*

In a bowl, mix together the yoghurt, rice and salt.

In a small tempering pan, add the clarified butter (*Ghee*) and put it on your heat source.

As soon as the clarified butter warms up, add the black mustard seeds, ginger, *chana dal* (split chick peas) and the curry leaves and let them all splutter and sizzle.

If adding carrot and green chillies, add it to the tempering pan at this point. Let the carrots cook a little.

Add to the rice and yoghurt mixture.

Your curd rice is ready.

Prep time: 5 minutes

Cooking time: 2 minutes

Total time: 7 minutes

## Lemon rice

This delicious twist on cooked rice too is a favourite dish in South India. Try this in the winters for the Vitamin C that lemon adds to this recipe.

*Ingredients*

Cooked rice-2 cups

Lemon juice-2 tablespoon

Clarified butter (*Ghee*) -1 tablespoon

Black Mustard-1/2 teaspoon

Ginger-1/2 inch piece chopped up finely

Curry leaves-a few

Deseeded chopped green chillies-1/2 teaspoon (this is only for flavour and not to make it hot)

Turmeric-1/2 teaspoon

Asafoetida (*Hing*)-a pinch

Roasted *Chana dal* (roasted split chick peas)-1/2 teaspoon

Water-2 tablespoon

Salt to taste

## Method

In a small wok (*kadhai*), add the clarified butter (*Ghee*) and put it on your heat source.

As soon as the clarified butter warms up, add the black mustard seeds, ginger, *chana dal* (split chick peas) and the curry leaves till they all splutter and sizzle.

Now add the green chillies, turmeric and asafoetida.

Add the rice, water and salt. Mix well.

Turn off your heat source and add the lemon juice.

Again Mix well.

Your lemon rice is ready.

Prep time: 5 minutes

Cooking time: 2 minutes

Total time: 7 minutes

## Tamarind rice

This unusually tangy dish too is an eternal favourite in South India.

*Ingredients*

Cooked rice-2 cups

Tamarind paste-1 tablespoon dissolved in half cup water

Jaggery-2 teaspoon

Clarified butter (*Ghee*) -1 tablespoon

Black Mustard-1/2 teaspoon

Ginger-1/2 inch piece chopped up finely

Curry leaves-a few

Deseeded chopped green chillies-1/2 teaspoon (this is only for flavour and not to make it hot)

Turmeric-1/2 teaspoon

Asafoetida (*Hing*)-a pinch

Roasted *Chana dal* (roasted split chick peas)-1/2 teaspoon

Salt to taste

*Method*

In a small wok (*kadhai*), add the clarified butter (*Ghee*) and put it on your heat source.

As soon as the clarified butter warms up, add the black mustard seeds, ginger, *chana dal* (split chick peas) and the curry leaves till they all splutter and sizzle.

Now add the green chillies, turmeric and asafoetida.

Add the tamarind paste and jaggery and let the jaggery dissolve.

Add the rice and salt. Mix well.

Turn off your heat source and let the tamarind paste and jaggery seep into the rice.

Your tamarind rice is ready.

Prep time: 5 minutes

Cooking time: 5 minutes

Total time: 10 minutes

## Tomato rice

If you find Tamarind Rice a little unusual for your taste buds, try this recipe which is also quite tangy.

*Ingredients*

Cooked rice-2 cups

Tomato puree-1/2 cup

Clarified butter (*Ghee*) -1 tablespoon

Fried Cashew nuts- 2 tablespoon

Black Mustard-1/2 teaspoon

Ginger-1/2 inch piece chopped up finely

Curry leaves-a few

Deseeded chopped green chillies-1/2 teaspoon (this is only for flavour and not to make it hot)

Turmeric-1/2 teaspoon

Asafoetida (*Hing*)-a pinch

Roasted *Chana dal* (roasted split chick peas)-1/2 teaspoon

Salt to taste

*Method*

In a small wok (*kadhai*), add the clarified butter (*Ghee)* and put it on your heat source.

As soon as the clarified butter warms up, add the black mustard seeds, ginger, *chana dal* (split chick peas) and the curry leaves till they all splutter and sizzle.

Now add the green chillies, turmeric and asafoetida.

Add the tomato puree and cook the puree for a few minutes.

Add the rice and salt. Mix well.

Turn off your heat source.

Sprinkle the cashew nuts on the rice.

Your tomato rice is ready.

Prep time: 5 minutes

Cooking time: 5 minutes

Total time: 10 minutes

## Onion Rice

This is the poor man's pulao made in a Jiffy. You can use this recipe to add some zing to your left over rice, the North Indian way.

*Ingredients*

Cooked rice-2 cups

Onion sliced- 2 medium size

Cumin seeds (*Jeera*)-1/2 teaspoon

Green Cardamom (*Chhoti elaichi*)-2

Cinnamon (*Dalchini*)-1/2 inch

Cloves (*Laung*)-4

Bay leaf (*Tejpatta*)-1

Clarified butter (*Ghee*)-1 tablespoon

Salt to taste

Sugar-1/4 teaspoon (dissolved in 2 tablespoon water)

*Method*

Place a small wok (*kadhai*) on your heat source.

Add the clarified butter (*Ghee*).

When the butter warms up, add the cumin seeds along with the cardamom, cinnamon, cloves and bay leaves. Stir a little.

As soon as it starts giving off a nice aroma, in less than a minute, add the onion slices. Do please make sure that the spices brown and not burn, otherwise your dish will be totally spoiled.

Fry till the onions become nicely golden brown.

Add the rice. Mix well.

Now, add the salt and the sugar which has already been dissolved in water. Stir again to mix well.

Switch off the heat source and take out the rice.

Enjoy!!!

Prep time: 5 minutes

Cooking time: 2 minutes

Total time: 7 minutes

## *Jeera Pulao* (Cumin Rice)

This is how the basic Indian pulao is made. If you master this, you can make any kind of pulao.

*Ingredients*

Long grain rice (Basmati)-1 cup

Water-2 cups

Cumin seeds (*Jeera*)-1/2 teaspoon

Green Cardamom (*Chhoti elaichi*)-2

Cinnamon (*Dalchini*)-1/2 inch

Cloves (*Laung*)-4

Bay leaf (*Tejpatta*)-1

Clarified butter (*Ghee*)-1 tablespoon

Salt to taste

Sugar-1/4 teaspoon

*Method*

Wash the rice well (*in a vessel 3-4 times, but don't rub it lest the grains break*) and let it naturally "dry", on an inclined plate, for 15-20 minutes. This helps enhance the aroma.

*If using a pressure cooker:*

In a pressure cooker, add the clarified butter and place it on your heat source.

When the butter warms up, add the cumin seeds along with the cardamom, cinnamon, cloves and bay leaves.

As soon as it starts giving a nice aroma, in less than a minute, add the rice along with the salt and sugar. Do please make sure that the spices brown and not burn, otherwise your dish will be totally spoiled.

Stir well.

Add the water.

Close the lid of the pressure cooker BUT remove the weight.

When steam starts escaping from the vent (don't worry, you will hear that typical sound), reduce the heat to minimum. In other words, if cooking on gas, turn the knob to SIM(mer).

Wait for 10 minutes and switch off the gas. Take out the rice.

Your hot fluffy *Jeera Pulao* is ready.

*If using a thick bottomed pan/vessel*

In a pan/vessel, add the clarified butter and place on fire.

When the butter warms up, add the cumin seeds along with the cardamom, cinnamon, cloves and bay leaves.

As soon as it starts giving a nice aroma in less than a minute, add the rice along with the salt and sugar. Do please make sure that the spices brown and not burn, otherwise your dish will be totally spoiled.

Stir well.

Add the water.

Cover the pan/vessel with a well-fitting lid.

Reduce the heat to minimum. In other words, if cooking on gas, turn the knob to SIM (mer). Let the rice cook for 15-20 minutes.

Switch off the heat source and let the rice remain in the vessel for another 5 minutes. Take out the rice.

Your hot fluffy *Jeera Pulao* is ready.

*If using a rice cooker*

In a pan/vessel, add the clarified butter and place on fire.

When the butter warms up, add the cumin seeds along with the cardamom, cinnamon, cloves and bay leaves.

As soon as it starts giving a nice aroma in less than a minute, add the rice along with the salt and sugar. Do please make sure that the spices brown and not burn, otherwise your dish will be totally spoiled.

Stir well.

Switch off the heat source and put all the ingredients into the rice cooker.

Add the water.

Switch on the rice cooker and the let the rice cook. The rice cooker will switch off on its own when the rice is cooked.

Prep time: 20 minutes

Cooking time: 12 minutes with a pressure cooker; 17-22 minutes with a deep pan; and as indicated in the rice cooker manual

Total time: 32 minutes with a pressure cooker; 37-42 minutes with a deep pan

## Saffron *pulao* (Saffron rice dish)

*Ingredients*

Long grain rice (Basmati)-1 cup

Water-2 cups

Black Cumin seeds (*Shahi Jeera*)-1/2 teaspoon

Green Cardamom (*Chhoti elaichi*)-2

Few strands of saffron dissolved in ¼ cup milk

Clarified butter (*Ghee*)-1 tablespoon

Salt to taste

Sugar-1/4 teaspoon

*Method*

Wash the rice well (*in a vessel 3-4 times, but don't rub it lest the grains break*) and let it naturally "dry", on an inclined plate, for 15-20 minutes. This helps enhance the aroma.

*If using a pressure cooker:*

In a pressure cooker, add the clarified butter and place it on your heat source.

When the butter warms up, add the cumin seeds along with the green cardamom.

As soon as it starts giving a nice aroma, in less than a minute, add the rice along with the salt and sugar. Do please make sure that the spices brown and not burn, otherwise your dish will be totally spoiled.

Stir well.

Add the water and saffron dissolved in milk.

Close the lid of the pressure cooker BUT remove the weight.

When steam starts escaping from the vent (don't worry, you will hear that typical sound), reduce the heat to minimum. In other words, if cooking on gas, turn the knob to SIM(mer).

Wait for 10 minutes and switch off the gas. Take out the rice.

Your hot fluffy Saffron *Pulao* is ready.

*If using a thick bottomed pan/vessel*

In a pan/vessel, add the clarified butter and place on fire.

When the butter warms up, add the cumin seeds along with the cardamom.

As soon as it starts giving a nice aroma in less than a minute, add the rice along with the salt and sugar. Do please make sure that the spices brown and not burn, otherwise your dish will be totally spoiled.

Stir well.

Add the water.

Cover the pan/vessel with a well-fitting lid.

Reduce the heat to minimum. In other words, if cooking on gas, turn the knob to SIM (mer). Let the rice cook for 15-20 minutes.

Switch off the heat source and let the rice remain in the vessel for another 5 minutes. Take out the rice.

Your hot fluffy Saffron *pulao* is ready.

*If using a rice cooker*

In a pan/vessel, add the clarified butter and place on fire.

When the butter warms up, add the cumin seeds along with the cardamom.

As soon as it starts giving a nice aroma in less than a minute, add the rice along with the salt and sugar. Do please make sure that the spices brown and not burn, otherwise your dish will be totally spoiled.

Stir well.

Switch off the heat source and put all the ingredients into the rice cooker.

Add the water.

Switch on the rice cooker and the let the rice cook. The rice cooker will switch off on its own when the rice is cooked.

Prep time: 20 minutes

Cooking time: 12 minutes with a pressure cooker; 17-22 minutes with a deep pan; and as indicated in the rice cooker manual

Total time: 32 minutes with a pressure cooker; 37-42 minutes with a deep pan

# Chapter 2

## Rice Cooked with Lentils

Please note that the dishes listed in this chapter do not come out well in a rice cooker. This is because all of the recipes need to have a little water and are not completely dry and may get overbrowned in a rice cooker.

### *Khichdi* (Mixture of Rice, Lentil and Veggies Dish)

*Khichdi* literally means a mixture. In some form or another, this is almost compulsorily prepared for the festival of *Makar Sakranti* that is celebrated all over India and Nepal. This festival is also known as *Pongal* in Tamil Nadu, *Bihu* in Assam, *Lohri* in Punjab or *Uttarayan* in Gujarat.

Interestingly, this is one of the few Hindu festivals that falls on the fixed day of 14 January, when the Sun moves from the Tropic of Capricorn to the Tropic of

Cancer heralding the arrival of spring and the beginning of the harvest season.

It is believed that on this day, Lord *Surya* (the Sun God) visits the house of his son *Shani* (Saturn), who is the lord of the *Makar rashi* (Capricorn) and the controller of the quantum of misfortune befalling humans. To appease *Shani*, therefore, many Indians prefer cooking *Khichdi* on Saturdays which is also known as *Shaniwar* or the day of Lord *Shani*.

*Khichdi* is otherwise the most nutritiously complete dish, consisting of carbs from rice, proteins from lentils and vitamins from veggies. Also it is quite a JIFFY dish.

*Ingredients*

Rice-3/4 cup

*Moong Dal* (Bengal Gram)-1/4 cup

Onion-1 (chopped up)

Ginger-1 inch

Spinach (only leaves)-500 grams or 18oz (2 cups) coarsely chopped

Peas--100 grams (3.5oz) (half cup)

Carrots-2 (cut into small pieces)

Tomato-1

*Khada* (that is, whole and not powdered) *Garam Masala* (Green cardamom--2, brown cardamom-1, Bay leaves-2, cinnamon stick-1/2 inch, black pepper-6, cloves-4, cumin seeds-1/2 tea spoon)

Coriander (Dhania) powder-1 teaspoon

Red chilli powder (only for flavour and not to make it hot)-1/4 teaspoon (you can add more if you like it hot)

Turmeric (*Haldi*)-1 teaspoon

Asafoetida (*Hing*)-1/4 teaspoon

*Ghee* (clarified butter)-2 tablespoon full

Salt- 1 level teaspoon roughly or to taste.

Water-3 cups (This will give your Khichdi a wet consistency. However, if you like your khichdi to be drier, then add only 2 cups of water instead of 3.)

*Method*

Wash the rice and dal together and let it dry for 5 minutes on an inclined plate.

*If using a pressure cooker:*

In a pressure cooker, put the clarified butter and put it on your heat source.

As it warms up, add the *Khada Garam Masala* and Asafoetida.

Let these all crackle but NOT burn.

Add the onion and ginger.

Sauté this for 2 minutes and then add the peas and the carrots.

Stir well.

Now add the coarsely chopped spinach, turmeric, coriander powder, red chilli powder and salt.

Add the rice, dal and the tomatoes.

Stir well.

Add the water and put the lid with the weight on the cooker.

After the cooker comes to full pressure, switch off the heat source but do NOT release the pressure.

Let the pressure cooker cool down by itself.

Open the cooker and you will find your *Khichdi* ready.

*If using a thick bottomed pan/vessel:*

In a pan/vessel, add the clarified butter and place it on your heat source.

When the butter warms up, add the *Khada Garam Masala* and Asafoetida (Hing).

Let these all crackle but NOT burn.

Add the onion and ginger.

Sauté this for 2 minutes.

Then add the peas and the carrots.

Stir well.

Then add the coarsely chopped spinach, turmeric, coriander powder, red chilli powder and salt.

Add the rice, dal and the tomatoes.

Stir well.

Add the water.

Cover the pan/vessel with a well-fitting lid.

Reduce the heat to minimum. In other words, if cooking on gas, turn the knob to SIM (mer). Let the *Khichdi* cook for 15-20 minutes.

Switch off the heat source and let the rice remain in the vessel for another 5 minutes.

Your *Khichdi* should now be ready.

Prep time: 5 minutes

Cooking time: 10 minutes with a pressure cooker; 20-25 minutes with a deep pan

Total time: 15 minutes with a pressure cooker; 25-30 minutes with a deep pan

## Chana Dal Khichdi (Rice dish cooked with split chick pea)

In this version of *Khichdi*, a different lentil viz. split chick pea (*Chana Dal*) is used in place of the more popular Bengal gram (*Moong Dal*). This imparts a very tasty twist to the humble Khichdi, which is worth a try.

*Ingredients*

Rice-1 cup

*Chana Dal* (Split Chick Pea)-1/4 cup

Onion-1 (chopped)

Garlic-2 cloves (chopped)

Ginger-1 inch (chopped)

Tomato-1

*Khada* (that is, whole and not powdered) *Garam Masala* (Green cardamom--2, brown cardamom-1, Bay leaves-2, cinnamon stick-1/2 inch, black pepper-6, cloves-4, cumin seeds-1/2 tea spoon)

Coriander (*Dhania*) powder-1 teaspoon

Red chilli powder (only for flavour and not to make it hot)-1/4 teaspoon (you can add more if you like it hot)

Turmeric (*Haldi*)-1 teaspoon

Asafoetida (*Hing*)-1/4 teaspoon

Desiccated coconut powder-2 tablespoon

*Ghee* (clarified butter)-2 tablespoon full

Salt- 1 level teaspoon roughly or to taste.

Water-3 cups

*Method*

Wash the rice and let it dry for 5 minutes on an inclined plate.

*If using a pressure cooker:*

In a pressure cooker, put the clarified butter and put it on your heat source.

As it warms up, add the *Khada Garam Masala* and Asafoetida.

Let these all crackle but NOT burn.

Add the onion, ginger and garlic.

Sauté this for 2 minutes and then add the washed *chana dal*.

Stir well.

Now add the turmeric, coriander powder, and red chilli powder.

Add the tomatoes.

Stir well.

Add the water and put the lid with the weight on the cooker.

After the cooker comes to full pressure, reduce the heat and let the *chana dal* cook for 7 minutes.

Switch off the heat source but do NOT release the pressure.

Let the pressure cooker cool down by itself.

Open the cooker and add the rice, desiccated coconut and salt.

Close the lid without the weight. As soon as the steam escapes, reduce the heat and let it cook for 10 minutes.

Your *Chana Dal Khichdi* is now ready.

*If using a thick bottomed pan/vessel:*

In a pan, put the clarified butter and put it on your heat source.

As it warms up, add the *Khada Garam Masala* and Asafoetida.

Let these all crackle but NOT burn.

Add the onion, ginger and garlic.

Sauté this for 2 minutes and then add the washed *chana dal*.

Stir well.

Now add the turmeric, coriander powder, and red chilli powder.

Add the tomatoes.

Stir well.

Add the water and reduce the heat. Cover the pan with the lid and let the *chana dal* cook for 25 minutes or till it becomes soft.

Open the lid and add the rice, desiccated coconut and salt.

In case the water has become less, you may want to add some more.

Close the lid again and as soon as the steam escapes, reduce the heat and let it cook for 10 minutes.

Your *Chana Dal Khichdi* is now ready.

Prep time: 10 minutes

Cooking time: 20 minutes with a pressure cooker; 50 minutes with a deep pan

Total time: 30 minutes with a pressure cooker; 60 minutes with a deep pan

## Light *Khichdi*

If you want to have something really light for a dinner, then instead of soups and salads, you may want to try out this recipe.

*Ingredients*

Rice-1 cup

*Dhuli Moong Dal* (Split Bengal Gram)-1/4 cup

*Dhuli Masoor Dal* (Split Red Lentils)-1/4 cup

Tomato-2

Turmeric (*Haldi*)-1/2 teaspoon

Cumin seeds (*Jeera*)-1/2 teaspoon

Clarified butter (*Ghee*)-2 tablespoon

Water-4 cups

Salt to taste

*Method*

Wash the rice and the *dals* together and let it dry for 5 minutes.

*If using a pressure cooker:*

In a pressure cooker, put the clarified butter and put it on your heat source.

As it warms up, add the cumin seeds (*jeera*).

Let this brown but NOT burn.

Add the rice, lentils, tomatoes and salt.

Stir well.

Add the water and put the lid with the weight on the cooker.

After the cooker comes to full pressure, reduce heat and let it cook for 5 minutes.

Switch off the heat source and let it cool on its own.

Open the cooker and you will find your Light *Khichdi* ready.

*If using a thick bottomed pan/vessel:*

In a pan, put the clarified butter and put it on your heat source.

As it warms up, add the cumin seeds (*jeera*).

Let this brown but NOT burn.

Add the rice, lentils, tomatoes and salt.

Stir well.

Add the water and cover the pan with lid and reduce the heat.

Let the *Khichdi* cook for about 35 minutes or till the rice and the lentils are well cooked and blended together.

If required you may add some more water.

Switch off the heat source.

Your Light *Khichdi* is ready.

Prep time: 5 minutes

Cooking time: 10 minutes with a pressure cooker; 40 minutes with a deep pan

Total time: 15 minutes with a pressure cooker; 45 minutes with a deep pan

## *Pongal*

This is the famous festival dish of South India, and quite a delicious twist on the North Indian Khichdi, I must say.

*Ingredients*

Rice-3/4 cup

*Moong Dal* (Bengal Gram)-1/4 cup

Curry Leaves-a few

Black Mustard Seeds (*Rai*)-1/2 teaspoon

Ginger-1 inch (2.5 cm or 1/3rd length of a finger) piece

Turmeric (*Haldi*)-1 teaspoon

Asafoetida (*Hing*)-1/4 teaspoon

*Ghee* (clarified butter)-2 tablespoon full

Salt- 1 level teaspoon roughly or to taste.

Water-3 cups

*Method*

Wash the rice and dal together and let it dry for 5 minutes on an inclined plate.

*If using a pressure cooker:*

In a pressure cooker, put the clarified butter and put it on your heat source.

As it warms up, add the Curry Leaves and Black Mustard Seeds.

As soon as it splutters, add the Asafoetida (*Hing*) and ginger.

Let this brown but NOT burn.

Now add the rice, dal, turmeric and the salt.

Stir well.

Add the water and put the lid with the weight on the cooker.

After the cooker comes to full pressure (*don't worry, you will hear that typical sound*), switch off the heat source but do NOT release the pressure.

Let the pressure cooker cool down by itself.

Open the cooker and you will find your *Pongal* ready.

*If using a thick bottomed pan/vessel:*

In a pan/vessel, add the clarified butter and place it on your heat source.

When the butter warms up, add the Curry Leaves and the Black Mustard Seeds.

As soon as it splutters, add the Asafoetida (*Hing*) and ginger.

Let this brown but NOT burn.

Now add the rice, *dal*, turmeric, and the salt.

Stir well.

Add the water.

Cover the pan/vessel with a well-fitting lid.

Reduce the heat to minimum. In other words, if cooking on gas, turn the knob to SIM (mer).

Let the *Pongal* cook for 15-20 minutes.

Switch off the heat source and let the rice remain in the vessel for another 5 minutes.

Your *Pongal* should now be ready.

Prep time: 5 minutes

Cooking time: 10 minutes with a pressure cooker; 20-25 minutes with a deep pan

Total time: 15 minutes with a pressure cooker; 25-30 minutes with a deep pan

## Bisi Belle Bhath

This is another classical recipe from South India, which I personally find to be the tastiest of all rice-lentil dishes that I have ever sampled.

Try this out only when you have a little more time and are in a somewhat adventurous mood.

*Ingredients*

*Arhar/Toor Dal* (Split Pigeon peas)-1/2 cup

Rice-1 cup

Water-4 cups

Turmeric-1/2 teaspoon

Coriander seeds (*Dhania*)-2 tablespoon

Asafoetida (*Hing*)-1/2 teaspoon

Dried Red Chilli-1 (de-seeded)

Cinnamon-1 small stick

Cloves-10

Freshly grated or desiccated coconut-3 tablespoon

Tamarind pulp dissolved in 2 tablespoon water-2 teaspoon

Black Mustard seeds (*Rai*)-1/2 teaspoon

Curry leaves-few

Desi *Ghee* (Clarified butter)-2 tablespoon

*Method*

*If using a pressure cooker:*

Wash the *Arhar/Toor dal* well and place it in the pressure cooker with turmeric, salt, cinnamon, cloves, asafoetida and water.

Place the cooker on a heat source and let it come to full pressure (*i.e. when the weight lifts and there is a whistling sound.*)

Reduce the heat and cook for 5 more minutes.

Meanwhile, i.e. while the lentils are cooking, wash the rice well *(in a vessel 3-4 times, but don't rub it lest the grains break)* and let it naturally "dry", on an inclined plate.

Remove the cooker from the heat source and open it.

Now, add the tamarind pulp to the cooked *dal* along with the coconut and rice.

Once more close the lid and put it on the heat source and let it come to full pressure.

Switch off the heat source and let the pressure cooker cool down itself.

In a small tempering pan, add the clarified butter. Once the clarified butter warms up, add the black mustard seeds, coriander seeds, curry leaves and red chilli.

The moment the mixture splutters (which takes only a few seconds), pour it over the cooked rice and dal dish.

Your *Bissi Belle Bhath* is ready.

*If using a thick bottomed deep pan/vessel:*

Wash the *Arhar/Toor dal* well and place in the pan with turmeric, salt, cinnamon, cloves, asafoetida and water.

Place the pan on a heat source and let the lentils cook till it is done.

Meanwhile, wash the rice well (*in a vessel 3-4 times, but don't rub it lest the grains break*) and let it naturally "dry", on an inclined plate.

Now, add the tamarind pulp to the cooked lentils along with the coconut and rice.

Close the pan with a tight fitting lid and put it on the heat source (with heat reduced to minimum).

Let the rice cook which should take about 15 minutes.

In a small tempering pan, add the clarified butter. Once the clarified butter warms up, add the black mustard seeds, coriander seeds, curry leaves and red chilli.

The moment the mixture splutters (which takes only a few seconds), pour it over the cooked rice and lentil dish.

Your *Bissi Belle Bhath* is ready.

Prep time: 5 minutes

Cooking time: 10 minutes with pressure cooker; 45 minutes with a deep pan

Total time: 20 minutes with a pressure cooker; 50 minutes with a deep pan

## Chapter 3

## Rice Cooked with Veggies

### *Mattar Pulao* (Peas Rice)

This is a simple rice dish that really goes well with any mutton or chicken curry.

*Ingredients*

Long grain rice (Basmati)-1 cup

Peas-1/2 cup

Sliced Onion-1 (Medium)

Water-2 cups

Cumin seeds (*Jeera*)-1/2 teaspoon

Green Cardamom (*Chhoti elaichi*)-2

Cinnamon (*Dalchini*)-1/2 inch

Cloves (*Laung*)-4

Bay leaf (*Tejpatta*)-1

Clarified butter (*Ghee*)-2 tablespoon

Salt to taste

Sugar-1/4 teaspoon

*Method*

Wash the rice well (*in a vessel 3-4 times, but don't rub it lest the grains break*) and let it naturally "dry", on an inclined plate, for 15-20 minutes. This helps enhance the aroma.

*If using a pressure cooker:*

In a pressure cooker, add the clarified butter and place it on your heat source.

When the butter warms up, add the cumin seeds along with the cardamom, cinnamon, cloves and bay leaves.

As soon as it starts giving a nice aroma, in less than a minute, add the onion slices and fry till translucent. Do please make sure that the spices brown and not burn, otherwise your dish will be totally spoiled.

Add the peas and stir for a minute.

Now add the rice along with the salt and sugar.

Stir well.

Add the water.

Close the lid of the pressure cooker BUT remove the weight.

When steam starts escaping from the vent (don't worry, you will hear that typical sound), reduce the heat to minimum. In other words, if cooking on gas, turn the knob to SIM (mer).

Wait for 10 minutes and switch off the gas.

Take out the rice.

Your pea *pulao* is ready.

*If using a thick bottomed pan/vessel:*

In a pan/vessel, add the clarified butter and place on fire.

When the butter warms up, add the cumin seeds along with the cardamom, cinnamon, cloves and bay leaves.

As soon as it starts giving a nice aroma, in less than a minute, add the onion slices and fry till translucent. Do please make sure that the spices brown and not burn, otherwise your dish will be totally spoiled.

Add the peas and stir for a minute.

Now add the rice along with the salt and sugar.

Stir well.

Add the water.

Cover the pan/vessel with a well-fitting lid.

Reduce the heat to minimum. In other words, if cooking on gas, turn the knob to SIM (mer). Let the rice cook for 15-20 minutes.

Switch off the heat source and let the rice remain in the vessel for another 5 minutes.

Take out the rice.

Your pea *pulao* is ready.

*If using a rice cooker*

In a pan/vessel, add the clarified butter and place on fire.

When the butter warms up, add the cumin seeds along with the cardamom, cinnamon, cloves and bay leaves.

As soon as it starts giving a nice aroma, in less than a minute, add the onion slices and fry till translucent. Do please make sure that the spices brown and not burn, otherwise your dish will be totally spoiled.

Add the peas and stir for a minute.

Now add the rice along with the salt and sugar.

Stir well.

Switch off the heat source and put all the ingredients into the rice cooker.

Add water.

Switch on the rice cooker and the let the rice cook. The rice cooker will switch off on its own when the rice is cooked.

Prep time: 20 minutes

Cooking time: 12 minutes with a pressure cooker; 17-22 minutes with a deep pan; and as indicated in the rice cooker manual

Total time: 32 minutes with a pressure cooker; 37-42 minutes with a deep pan

## Dry Fruits *Pulao*

This is a rich pilaf dish, fit enough to be on a grand Moghul's table.

*Ingredients*

Long grain rice (Basmati)-1 cup

Water-2 cups

Black Cumin seeds (*Shahi Jeera*)-1/2 teaspoon

Green Cardamom (*Chhoti elaichi*)-2

Few strands of saffron dissolved in ¼ cup milk

Raisins-2 tablespoon

Blanched almonds-3 tablespoon

*(To blanch almonds, immerse them in half a cup of hot water for 30 minutes. Remove the skin thereafter.)*

Roasted Cashew nuts-3 tablespoon

*(The method to roast the cashew nuts: in a small pan, add about a tablespoon of cooking oil. Put the pan on your heat source. When the oil heats up, add the cashew nuts and stir till they turn golden. Immediately remove the cashew nuts to a plate. Remember if you leave the cashew nuts in the pan, the hot oil will keep roasting the cashew nuts and burn them.)*

Clarified butter (*Ghee*)-1 tablespoon

Salt to taste

Sugar-1/4 teaspoon

*Method*

Wash the rice well (*in a vessel 3-4 times, but don't rub it lest the grains break*) and let it naturally "dry", on an inclined plate, for 15-20 minutes. This helps enhance the aroma.

*If using a pressure cooker:*

In a pressure cooker, add the clarified butter and place it on your heat source.

When the butter warms up, add the cumin seeds along with the green cardamom.

As soon as it starts giving a nice aroma, in less than a minute, add the rice along with the salt and sugar. Do please make sure that the spices brown and not burn, otherwise your dish will be totally spoiled.

Add the raisins and the blanched almonds.

Stir well.

Add the water and saffron dissolved in milk.

Close the lid of the pressure cooker BUT remove the weight.

When steam starts escaping from the vent (don't worry, you will hear that typical sound), reduce the heat to minimum. In other words, if cooking on gas, turn the knob to SIM(mer).

Wait for 10 minutes and switch off the gas. Take out the rice.

Your hot fluffy Dry Fruits *Pulao* is ready.

Before serving, sprinkle the roasted cashew nuts on the pulao and enjoy.

*If using a thick bottomed pan/vessel*

In a pan/vessel, add the clarified butter and place on fire.

When the butter warms up, add the cumin seeds along with the cardamom.

As soon as it starts giving a nice aroma in less than a minute, add the rice along with the salt and sugar. Do please make sure that the spices brown and not burn, otherwise your dish will be totally spoiled.

Add the raisins and the blanched almonds.

Stir well.

Add the water.

Cover the pan/vessel with a well-fitting lid.

Reduce the heat to minimum. In other words, if cooking on gas, turn the knob to SIM (mer). Let the rice cook for 15-20 minutes.

Switch off the heat source and let the rice remain in the vessel for another 5 minutes. Take out the rice.

Your hot fluffy Dry Fruits *pulao* is ready.

Before serving, sprinkle the roasted cashew nuts on the pulao and enjoy.

*If using a rice cooker*

In a pan/vessel, add the clarified butter and place on fire.

When the butter warms up, add the cumin seeds along with the cardamom.

As soon as it starts giving a nice aroma in less than a minute, add the rice along with the salt and sugar. Do please make sure that the spices brown and not burn, otherwise your dish will be totally spoiled.

Add the raisins and the blanched almonds.

Stir well.

Switch off the heat source and put all the ingredients into the rice cooker.

Add the water.

Switch on the rice cooker and the let the rice cook. The rice cooker will switch off on its own when the rice is cooked.

Before serving, sprinkle the roasted cashew nuts on the pulao and enjoy.

Prep time: 20 minutes

Cooking time: 12 minutes with a pressure cooker; 17-22 minutes with a deep pan; and as indicated in the rice cooker manual

Total time: 32 minutes with a pressure cooker; 37-42 minutes with a deep pan

## Mixed Vegetable Cheese *Biryani*

Who says vegetarians can't enjoy *Biryanis*? Try this dish and I guarantee you the same flavours as of any normal non-vegetarian *Biryani* and almost the same protein levels (that are brought in by the tofu or paneer).

*Ingredients*

Long grain rice (Basmati)-2 cups

Cottage Cheese (*Paneer*) or Tofu-200 grams (7oz) (1 cup)

Peas-1/4 cup

Carrots cut into small pieces-1/4 cup

Cauliflower florets-1/4 cup

Beans-1/4 cup

Blanched Almonds-2 tablespoon

*(To blanch almonds, immerse them in half a cup of hot water for 30 minutes. Remove the skin thereafter.)*

Sliced Onion-1 (Medium)

Chopped Ginger-1 inch piece

Chopped Garlic-4 cloves

Turmeric (*Haldi*)-1/2 teaspoon

Red Chilli powder-1/4 teaspoon

Coriander powder-1 teaspoon

*Garam Masala* (mixture of common Indian spices) - 1/2 teaspoon

Tip: If you can't get ready-made garam masala mixture from a nearby Indian store, you can make yours by using 1 black cardamom, 3 green cardamoms, 4 cloves, and 1 inch cinnamon-all ground together for this dish.

Red Tomatoes pureed-2

Cumin seeds (*Jeera*)-1/2 teaspoon

Clarified butter (*Ghee*)-4 tablespoon

Salt to taste

Sugar-1/4 teaspoon

Water-4 cups

*Method*

Wash the rice well (*in a vessel 3-4 times, but don't rub it lest the grains break*) and let it naturally "dry", on an inclined plate, for 15-20 minutes. This helps enhance the aroma.

Roast the cottage cheese (*paneer*) or tofu on a dry pan and then cut into bite size pieces.

*If using a pressure cooker:*

In a pressure cooker, add the clarified butter and place it on your heat source.

When the butter warms up, add the cumin seeds. As soon as it starts giving a nice aroma, in less than a minute, add the onion slices and fry till translucent. Do please make sure that the spices brown and not burn, otherwise your dish will be totally spoiled.

Add the ginger and garlic. Stir for a minute.

Add all the vegetables except the *Paneer* (cottage cheese) and stir well.

Now add the turmeric, chilli powder, coriander and *garam masala* and again stir well.

Pour the tomato puree over this mixture and stir till the tomatoes give off a nice aroma. That's the indication that they are getting cooked.

Add now the *paneer* (or tofu) and the blanched almonds.

Add the salt and sugar. Now add the rice.

Stir well.

Add the water.

Close the lid of the pressure cooker BUT remove the weight.

When steam starts escaping from the vent (*don't worry, you will hear that typical sound*), reduce the heat to minimum. In other words, if cooking on gas, turn the knob to SIM (mer).

Wait for 10 minutes and switch off the gas.

Take out the rice. Your Vegetable *biryani* is ready.

This is a complete meal in itself.

*If using a thick bottomed pan/vessel:*

In a pan/vessel, add the clarified butter and place on fire.

When the butter warms up, add the cumin seeds. As soon as it starts giving a nice aroma, in less than a minute, add the onion slices and fry till translucent. Do please make sure that the spices brown and not burn, otherwise your dish will be totally spoiled.

Add the ginger and garlic. Stir for a minute.

Add all the vegetables except the *Paneer* (cottage cheese) and stir well.

Now add the turmeric, chilli powder, coriander and *garam masala* and again stir well.

Pour the tomato puree over this mixture and stir till the tomatoes give off a nice aroma. That's the indication that they are getting cooked.

Add now the *paneer* (or tofu) and the blanched almonds.

Add the salt and sugar. Now add the rice.

Stir well.

Add the water.

Cover the pan/vessel with a well-fitting lid.

Reduce the heat to minimum. In other words, if cooking on gas, turn the knob to SIM (mer).

Let the rice cook for 20-25 minutes. Please check that the rice has cooked well.

Switch off the heat source and let the rice remain in the vessel for another 5 minutes.

Take out the rice. Your Vegetable *biryani* is ready.

*If using a rice cooker*

In a pan/vessel, add the clarified butter and place on fire.

When the butter warms up, add the cumin seeds. As soon as it starts giving a nice aroma, in less than a minute, add the onion slices and fry till translucent. Do please make sure that the spices brown and not burn, otherwise your dish will be totally spoiled.

Add the ginger and garlic. Stir for a minute.

Add all the vegetables except the *Paneer* (cottage cheese) and stir well.

Now add the turmeric, chilli powder, coriander and *garam masala* and again stir well.

Pour the tomato puree over this mixture and stir till the tomatoes give off a nice aroma. That's the indication that they are getting cooked.

Add now the *paneer* (or tofu) and the blanched almonds.

Add the salt and sugar. Now add the rice.

Stir well.

Switch off the heat source and put all the ingredients into the rice cooker.

Add the water.

Switch on the rice cooker and the let the rice cook. The rice cooker will switch off on its own when the rice is cooked.

Prep time: 20 minutes

Cooking time: 12 minutes with a pressure cooker; 20-25 minutes with a deep thick bottomed pan; and as indicated in the rice cooker manual

Total time: 32 minutes with a pressure cooker; 40-45 minutes with a deep thick bottomed pan

## *Navratna Pulao* (Nine Jewels Rice dish)

This is the ultimate vegetarian pilaf dish. Savour this on those really special occasions.

*Ingredients*

Long grain rice (Basmati)-2 cups

Cottage Cheese (*Paneer*) or Tofu-200 grams (7oz) (1 cup)

Peas-1/4 cup

Carrots cut into small pieces-1/4 cup

Cauliflower florets-1/4 cup

Raisins-2 tablespoon

*Roasted Cashew nuts-3 tablespoon (The method to roast the cashew nuts: in a small pan, add about a tablespoon of cooking oil. Put the pan on your heat source. When the oil heats up, add the cashew nuts and stir till they turn golden. Immediately remove the cashew nuts to a plate. Remember if you leave the cashew nuts in the pan, the hot oil will keep roasting the cashew nuts and burn them.)*

Sliced Onion-1 (Medium)

Chopped Ginger-1 inch piece

Black Cumin seeds (*Shahi Jeera*)-1/2 teaspoon

Green Cardamom (*Chhoti elaichi*)-2

Brown Cardamom (*Badi elaichi*)-1

Cinnamon (*Dalchini*)-1/2 inch

Cloves (*Laung*)-4

Star aniseed-1

Mace (*Javitri*)-One small piece

Bay leaf (*Tejpatta*)-1

Clarified butter (*Ghee*)-4 tablespoon

Salt to taste

Sugar-1/2 teaspoon

Few strands of saffron dissolved in ¼ cup milk

Water-4 cups

*Method*

Wash the rice well (*in a vessel 3-4 times, but don't rub it lest the grains break*) and let it naturally "dry", on an inclined plate, for 15-20 minutes. This helps enhance the aroma.

Roast the cottage cheese (*paneer*) or tofu on a dry pan and then cut into bite size pieces.

In a pan, add 2 tablespoon of clarified butter and gently roast peas, carrots and cauliflower one by one and keep aside.

*If using a pressure cooker:*

In a pressure cooker, add the clarified butter and place it on your heat source.

When the butter warms up, add the black cumin seeds along with the green cardamom, brown cardamom, cinnamon, cloves, star aniseed, mace and bay leaf.

As soon as these all start giving a nice aroma, in less than a minute, add the onion slices and fry till translucent. Do please make sure that the spices brown and not burn, otherwise your dish will be totally spoiled.

Add the ginger and stir for a minute.

Now add the rice along with the salt and sugar.

Stir well.

Add the roasted vegetables along with the *paneer* (cottage cheese) or tofu and again stir well.

Add the water, raisins and the saffron dissolved in milk.

Close the lid of the pressure cooker BUT remove the weight.

When steam starts escaping from the vent (*don't worry, you will hear that typical sound*), reduce the heat to minimum. In other words, if cooking on gas, turn the knob to SIM (mer).

Wait for 10 minutes and switch off the gas.

Take out the rice. Your *Navratna pulao* is ready.

Before serving, sprinkle some roasted cashew nuts on the pulao and enjoy.

*If using a thick bottomed pan/vessel:*

In a pan/vessel, add the clarified butter and place on fire.

When the butter warms up, add the black cumin seeds along with the green cardamom, brown cardamom, cinnamon, cloves, star aniseed, mace and bay leaf.

As soon as these all start giving a nice aroma, in less than a minute, add the onion slices and fry till translucent.

Do please make sure that the spices brown and not burn, otherwise your dish will be totally spoiled.

Add the ginger and stir for a minute.

Now add the rice along with the salt and sugar.

Stir well.

Add the roasted vegetables along with the *paneer* (cottage cheese) or tofu and again stir well.

Add the water, raisins and the saffron dissolved in milk.

Cover the pan/vessel with a well-fitting lid.

Reduce the heat to minimum. In other words, if cooking on gas, turn the knob to SIM (mer). Let the rice cook for 20-25 minutes. Please check that the rice has cooked well.

Switch off the heat source and let the rice remain in the vessel for another 5 minutes.

Take out the rice. Your *Navratna pulao* is ready.

Before serving, sprinkle some roasted cashew nuts on the pulao and enjoy.

*If using a rice cooker*

In a pan/vessel, add the clarified butter and place on fire.

When the butter warms up, add the black cumin seeds along with the green cardamom, brown cardamom, cinnamon, cloves, star aniseed, mace and bay leaf.

As soon as these all start giving a nice aroma, in less than a minute, add the onion slices and fry till translucent.

Do please make sure that the spices brown and not burn, otherwise your dish will be totally spoiled.

Add the ginger and stir for a minute.

Now add the rice along with the salt and sugar.

Stir well.

Add the roasted vegetables along with the *paneer* (cottage cheese) or tofu and again stir well.

Add the water, raisins and the saffron dissolved in milk.

Switch off the heat source and put all the ingredients into the rice cooker.

Switch on the rice cooker and the let the rice cook. The rice cooker will switch off on its own when the rice is cooked.

Take out the rice. Your *Navratna pulao* is ready.

Before serving, sprinkle some roasted cashew nuts on the pulao and enjoy.

Prep time: 20 minutes

Cooking time: 12 minutes with a pressure cooker; 20-25 minutes with a deep thick bottomed pan; and as indicated in the rice cooker manual

Total time: 32 minutes with a pressure cooker; 40-45 minutes with a deep thick bottomed pan

## Stir Fried Rice

Try this dish when you have some left-over boiled rice lying around, and you will be pleasantly surprised at the transformation.

*Ingredients*

Cooked Boiled rice-1 cup

Cauliflower-a few florets

Broccoli-1 small

Carrot-1

French beans-a few

Peas- ¼ cup

Button Mushrooms-4

Chopped Onions-2

Chopped Garlic-4 cloves

Chopped Ginger-1 inch

Red Chilli Powder-1/4 teaspoon

*Garam Masala* (mixture of common Indian spices) - 1/4 teaspoon

*Tip: If you can't get ready-made garam masala mixture from a nearby Indian store, you can make yours by using 1 black cardamom, 3 green*

*cardamoms, 4 cloves, and 1 inch cinnamon-all ground together for this dish.*

Turmeric (*Haldi*)-1/4 teaspoon

Egg-1

Salt to taste

Cooking Oil- 1 + ½ tablespoon (1 tablespoon for cooking vegetables + ½ tablespoon for the egg)

*Method*

Wash the vegetables and chop into small pieces.

In a wok, add the cooking oil and as soon as it warms up, add the chopped onions, garlic cloves and ginger.

As soon as the mixture starts giving off a nice aroma, add the vegetables.

Stir well.

Cover the wok, reduce the flame and let the vegetables steam in their own juice till cooked.

You may add the salt at this juncture along with turmeric, red chilli powder and *garam masala*.

Stir well.

Add the boiled rice, and again stir well so that all the ingredients are well mixed.

Switch off the heat source.

In a separate pan, pour the half tablespoon oil. While the oil heats up, beat the egg in a bowl. Pour the egg batter into the pan and let it cook like an omelette.

Remove the omelette from the pan and cut into strips.

Sprinkle this egg over your fried rice.

Your fried rice is ready.

Prep time: 10 minutes

Cooking time: 20 minutes

Total time: 30 minutes

# Chapter 4

## Rice Cooked with Meats

Rice is a great neutral medium to cook all kinds of meats with. We present five basic recipes, which once mastered can be used to rustle up myriad variations.

### Prawn Stir Fried Rice

*Ingredients*

Cooked Boiled rice-1 cup

De-shelled Prawns-200 grams (7oz) (1 cup)

Chopped Onion-1

Chopped Red Pepper-1

Chopped Garlic-4 cloves

Tomato Puree-2 tablespoon

Soya Sauce-1 + ½ tablespoon

Vinegar-1/2 teaspoon

Red Chilli sauce-1/2 teaspoon

Sugar-1/2 teaspoon

Salt to taste

Cooking Oil- 2 tablespoon

*Method*

Marinate the prawns with some salt, half tablespoon soya sauce and ¼ teaspoon red chilli sauce. Leave the prawns for 15 minutes.

In a wok, add 1 tablespoon cooking oil and as soon as it warms up, add the marinated prawns and sauté till the prawns are cooked.

Remove from the wok and keep the sauté prawns aside.

Now, add another tablespoon of cooking oil to the same wok and add the chopped garlic cloves.

As soon as the garlic starts giving off a nice aroma, add the chopped onions and sauté till the onion becomes translucent. Add the chopped red pepper.

Stir well.

Now add rest of the soya sauce, the red chilli sauce, the vinegar and the tomato puree. Also, add ½ teaspoon sugar and salt for the rice. Stir well.

Add the boiled rice, and again stir well so that all the ingredients are well mixed.

Now add the prawns and again stir well. Switch off the heat source.

Your prawn fried rice is ready.

Prep time: 10 minutes

Cooking time: 20 minutes

Total time: 30 minutes

## Chicken *Biryani*

*Biryanis* are normally elaborate affairs with saffron-tinged rice layered with cooked meats and then cooked in a pot sealed with dough. We present here, however, our Home- Style JIFFY version, which is in my opinion also tastier.

*Ingredients*

*For the chicken:*

Whole chicken -1 (cut into 8 pieces)

Chopped Onion-3 large

Chopped Ginger-2 inch piece

Chopped Garlic-8 Cloves

Tomatoes-2

Yoghurt-1 tablespoon

Coriander powder-2 teaspoon

*Garam Masala*-1 teaspoon

Tip: If you can't get ready-made *garam masala* mixture from a nearby Indian store, you can make yours by using 1 black cardamom, 3 green cardamoms, 4 cloves, and 1 inch cinnamon-all ground together for this dish.

Red chilli powder-1/4 teaspoon (enough only to add flavour and not to make it hot)

Cumin seeds-1/2 teaspoon

Cooking Oil-2 tablespoon

*Ghee* (Clarified butter)-1 tablespoon

Water-1/2 or 1 cup (just to ensure that the chicken cooks and doesn't burn)

Salt to taste

*For the rice:*

Long grain rice (Basmati)-2 cups

Chicken stock-4 cups

Black Cumin seeds (*Shahi Jeera*)-1/2 teaspoon

Green Cardamom (*Chhoti elaichi*)-4

Brown Cardamom (*Badi elaichi*)-2

Cinnamon (*Dalchini*)-1 inch

Cloves (*Laung*)-6

Bay leaf (*Tejpatta*)-1

Clarified butter (*Ghee*)-1 tablespoon

Salt to taste

Sugar-1/2 teaspoon

Few strands of saffron dissolved in ¼ cup warm milk

Blanched Almonds-24 kernels

*(To blanch almonds, immerse them in half a cup of hot water for 30 minutes. Remove the skin thereafter.)*

*Method*

First of all, wash the rice well (*in a vessel 3-4 times, but don't rub it lest the grains break*) and let it naturally "dry", on an inclined plate, for 15-20 minutes. This helps enhance the aroma.

Next, prepare the chicken stock. Put in a vessel, the neck and wings of the chicken and pour 4 cups of water over it. Now add ½ inch piece of cinnamon, one green cardamom, and two cloves.

If using pressure cooker, cook under full pressure for 5 minutes.

If not using a pressure cooker then let the stock be made for half an hour on low heat.

Remove the chicken pieces, strain and keep the stock ready.

*Now, prepare the chicken:*

In a pressure cooker, add the oil and the put it on your heat source.

As the oil turns hot, add the cumin seeds and let it splutter.

Immediately add the chopped onion.

Stir well till the onions become translucent.

Now, add the chopped ginger and garlic and stir till it starts giving off a nice aroma.

Add the chicken and the *ghee* (clarified butter).

Stir well.

Add the coriander powder, *garam masala* and the red chilli powder.

Stir and cook the chicken till all the water evaporates and the chicken becomes almost dry. This ensures that all the raw flavours of chicken, onions, etc. are removed.

Add now the tomatoes and the yoghurt.

Stir well again and add the salt.

Let the tomatoes cook well.

Now, add the water, and close the lid of the pressure cooker with weight.

Let it come to full pressure *(i.e. when the weight lifts and there is a whistling sound).*

Turn the heat to low and cook for another 5 minutes.

Remove the weight from the cooker and dry the chicken completely in the open cooker itself.

If not using a pressure cooker, then cook till the chicken is cooked thoroughly and dried.

Separately, in a wok, add the clarified butter along with black cumin seeds, green cardamom, brown cardamom, cinnamon, cloves and bay leaves.

As soon as you start getting a nice aroma, in less than a minute, add the rice along with the salt and sugar.

Do please ensure that the spices brown and not burn, otherwise your dish will be totally spoiled.

Stir well.

Now, add the rice to the cooked chicken in the pressure cooker.

Add the chicken stock, the saffron dissolved in milk and the blanched almonds.

Gently stir so that the mixture is well blended but the rice doesn't break.

Now, close the lid of the pressure cooker without the weight and place on the heat source.

As soon as the steam starts escaping, reduce the heat to low and let it cook for 10 minutes.

Switch off the heat source and let the cooker cool for about 10 minutes before you open it.

This helps all the flavours to seep into the rice and the chicken.

That's all. Your delicious chicken *biryani* is ready.

In case not using a pressure cooker, then place the cooked chicken and the prepared rice in a deep thick bottomed vessel along with the chicken stock, saffron and almonds.

Gently stir and then place the vessel on the heat source.

As soon as the stock starts boiling, reduce the heat source and close with a tight fitting lid.

The *biryani* should be ready in about 15 minutes but you should check by pressing one grain of rice to see if the rice has been properly cooked.

After switching off the heat source, leave the biryani inside the deep pan with the lid tightly shut for another 10 minutes. This helps all the flavours to seep into the rice and the chicken.

*If using a rice cooker*

First of all, wash the rice well (*in a vessel 3-4 times, but don't rub it lest the grains break*) and let it naturally "dry", on an inclined plate, for 15-20 minutes. This helps enhance the aroma.

Next, prepare the chicken stock. Put in a vessel, the neck and wings of the chicken and pour 4 cups of water over it. Now add ½ inch piece of cinnamon, one green cardamom, and two cloves.

If using pressure cooker, cook under full pressure for 5 minutes.

If not using a pressure cooker then let the stock be made for half an hour on low heat.

Remove the chicken pieces and keep the stock ready.

*Now, prepare the chicken:*

In a pressure cooker, add the oil and the put it on your heat source.

As the oil turns hot, add the cumin seeds and let it splutter.

Immediately add the chopped onion.

Stir well till the onions become translucent.

Now, add the chopped ginger and garlic and stir till it starts giving off a nice aroma.

Add the chicken and the *ghee* (clarified butter).

Stir well.

Add the coriander powder, *garam masala* and the red chilli powder.

Stir and cook the chicken till all the water evaporates and the chicken becomes almost dry. This ensures that all the raw flavours of chicken, onions, etc. are removed.

Add now the tomatoes and the yoghurt.

Stir well again and add the salt.

Let the tomatoes cook well.

Now, add the water, and close the lid of the pressure cooker with weight.

Let it come to full pressure (*i.e. when the weight lifts and there is a whistling sound*).

Turn the heat to low and cook for another 5 minutes.

Remove the weight from the cooker and dry the chicken completely in the open cooker itself.

If not using a pressure cooker, then cook till the chicken is cooked thoroughly and dried.

Separately, in a wok, add the clarified butter along with black cumin seeds, green cardamom, brown cardamom, cinnamon, cloves and bay leaves.

As soon as you start getting a nice aroma, in less than a minute, add the rice along with the salt and sugar.

Do please ensure that the spices brown and not burn, otherwise your dish will be totally spoiled.

Stir well.

Now, add the rice to the cooked chicken.

Switch off the heat source and put all the ingredients into the rice cooker.

Add the chicken stock, the saffron dissolved in milk and the blanched almonds.

Gently stir so that the mixture is well blended but the rice doesn't break.

Switch on the rice cooker and the let the rice cook. The rice cooker will switch off on its own when the rice is cooked.

Prep time: 30 minutes

Cooking time: 25 minutes with a pressure cooker; 60 minutes with a deep pan; and as indicated in the rice cooker manual

Total time: 55 minutes with a pressure cooker; 90 minutes with a deep pan

## Hyderabadi Chicken *Biryani*

*Ingredients*

Whole chicken -1 (cut into 8 pieces)

Chopped Onion-3 large

Chopped Ginger-2 inch piece

Chopped Garlic-8 Cloves

Tomatoes-2

Yoghurt-1 tablespoon

Coriander powder-2 teaspoon

*Garam Masala*-1 teaspoon

Tip: If you can't get ready-made *garam masala mixture* from a nearby Indian store, you can make yours by using 1 black cardamom, 3 green cardamoms, 4 cloves, and 1 inch cinnamon-all ground together for this dish.

Red chilli powder-1/4 teaspoon (enough only to add flavour and not to make it hot)

Cumin seeds-1/2 teaspoon

Cooking Oil-2 tablespoon

*Ghee* (Clarified butter)-1 tablespoon

Water-1/2 or 1 cup (just to ensure that the chicken cooks and doesn't burn)

Cooked rice with a little salt and a teaspoon *ghee* (clarified butter)-3 cups

Saffron-a few strands dissolved in one fourth cup milk

Blanched and fried Almonds-3 tablespoon

*(To blanch almonds, immerse them in half a cup of hot water for 30 minutes. Remove the skin thereafter and fry till a light golden colour is achieved.)*

Salt to taste

*Method*

In a pressure cooker, add the oil and the put it on your heat source.

As the oil turns hot, add the cumin seeds and let it splutter.

Immediately add the chopped onion.

Stir well till the onions become translucent.

Now, add the chopped ginger and garlic and stir till it starts giving off a nice aroma.

Add the chicken and the *ghee* (clarified butter).

Stir well.

Add the coriander powder, *garam masala* and red chilli powder.

Stir and cook the chicken till all the water evaporates and the chicken becomes almost dry. This process ensures that all the raw flavours of chicken, onions, etc. are removed.

Add now the tomatoes and the yoghurt.

Stir well again and add the salt.

Let the tomatoes cook well.

Now, add the water, and close the lid of the pressure cooker with weight.

Let it come to full pressure (*i.e. when the weight lifts and there is a whistling sound*).

Turn the heat to low and cook for another 5 minutes.

If not using a pressure cooker, then cook till the chicken is cooked thoroughly.

Remove the weight from the cooker and dry the chicken completely in the open cooker itself.

Layer a deep pan with rice and chicken pieces with the gravy alternatively.

Finally cover with rice and pour the saffron and milk over it.

Sprinkle the almonds.

Cover with an aluminium foil and place it in the oven at 150 degrees C (302 degrees F) for 15 minutes.

Prep time: 30 minutes

Cooking time: 40 minutes with a pressure cooker; 75 minutes with a deep pan

Total time: 70 minutes with a pressure cooker; 105 minutes with a deep pan

## Chicken *Kofta* (Mince ball) *Biryani*

*Ingredients*

For the chicken *Kofta* (Mince balls):

Chicken mince -1/2 Kg (18oz) (2 cups)

Onion-2 large (chopped)

Ginger-2 inch piece

Garlic-8 Cloves

Tomatoes-3 (chopped)

(Onion + Ginger + Garlic + Tomatoes blended and made into a fine paste)

Coriander powder-2 teaspoon

Turmeric-1 teaspoon

*Garam Masala*-1+1/2 teaspoon

Tip: If you can't get ready-made *garam masala mixture* from a nearby Indian store, you can make yours by using 2 black cardamom, 4 green cardamoms, 6 cloves, and 1.5 inch cinnamon-all ground together for this dish.

Red chilli powder-1/4 teaspoon (enough only to add flavour and not to make it spicy)

Cumin seeds-1/2 teaspoon

Cooking Oil-3 tablespoon

*Ghee* (Clarified butter)-1 tablespoon

Water-1/2 cup

Bread-2 slices soaked in water

Egg-1

Salt to taste

For the rice:

Long grain rice (Basmati)-2 cups

Chicken stock-4 cups

Black Cumin seeds (*Shahi Jeera*)-1/2 teaspoon

Green Cardamom (*Chhoti elaichi*)-4

Brown Cardamom (*Badi elaichi*)-2

Cinnamon (*Dalchini*)-1 inch

Cloves (*Laung*)-6

Bay leaf (*Tejpatta*)-1

Clarified butter (*Ghee*)-1 tablespoon

Salt to taste

Sugar-1/2 teaspoon

Few strands of saffron dissolved in ¼ cup milk

Blanched Almonds-24 kernels

*(To blanch almonds, immerse them in half a cup of hot water for 30 minutes. Remove the skin thereafter.)*

*Method*

First of all, wash the rice well (*in a vessel 3-4 times, but don't rub it lest the grains break*) and let it naturally "dry", on an inclined plate, for 15-20 minutes. This helps enhance the aroma.

Next, prepare the chicken stock. Take the neck and wings of the chicken and pour 4 cups of water over it along with ½ inch piece of cinnamon, one green cardamom, and two cloves. If using pressure cooker, cook under full pressure for 5 minutes. If not using a pressure cooker then let the stock be made for half an hour on low heat.

Remove the chicken pieces, strain and keep the stock ready.

*Now, prepare the chicken Kofta:*

In a bowl, mix together the chicken mince, one egg, half teaspoon *garam masala* and salt.

Add the bread slices after squeezing out all the water.

Make into walnut size balls.

In a frying pan, add the cooking oil and gently fry these balls 2-3 at a time and keep it in a plate.

Switch off the heat source.

In a pressure cooker, pour the oil from the pan and put it on your heat source.

As the oil turns hot, add the cumin seeds and let it splutter.

Immediately add the Onion + Ginger + Garlic + Tomatoes fine paste.

Stir well till the paste starts giving off a nice aroma and you can see the oil ooze out from the sides.

Add the coriander powder, turmeric, remaining 1 spoon of *garam masala* and red chilli powder.

Stir well again and add the salt.

Now, add the water.

As the mixture comes to a boil, gently add the fried chicken mince balls.

Close the lid of the pressure cooker with weight and let it come to full pressure (*i.e. when the weight lifts and there is a whistling sound*).

Immediately reduce the heat (to SIM on a gas stove) and let the chicken mince balls cook for 2 more minutes before turning off the heat source.

Let the cooker cool down on its own.

In case you are using a wok/deep pan, cover that with a tight fitting lid and cook for about 20 minutes or till the *Koftas* are completely cooked.

Now, add the rice to the cooked chicken *Kofta* in the pressure cooker.

Add the chicken stock and the saffron dissolved in milk and the blanched almonds.

Gently stir so that the mixture is well blended but the rice or the *Koftas* don't break.

Now, close the lid of the pressure cooker without the weight and place on the heat source.

As soon as the steam starts escaping, reduce the heat to low and let it cook for 10 minutes.

Switch off the heat source thereafter and let the cooker cool for about 10 minutes before opening the same. This helps all the flavours to seep into the rice and the chicken *kofta*.

That's all. Your delicious chicken *Kofta* biryani is ready.

In case not using a pressure cooker, then place the cooked chicken *Koftas* and the prepared rice in a deep thick bottomed vessel along with the chicken stock, saffron and almonds.

Gently stir and then place the vessel on the heat source.

As soon as the stock starts boiling, reduce the heat source and close with a tight fitting lid.

The *biryani* should be ready in about 15 minutes but you should check by pressing one grain of rice to see if the rice has been properly cooked.

After switching off the heat source, leave the biryani inside the deep pan with the lid tightly shut for another 10 minutes. This helps all the flavours to seep into the rice and the chicken.

*If using a rice cooker*

Place the cooked chicken *koftas* and the prepared rice in to the rice cooker.

Add the chicken stock, saffron and almonds.

Stir gently.

Switch on the rice cooker and the let the rice cook. The rice cooker will switch off on its own when the rice is cooked.

Prep time: 15 minutes

Cooking time: 15 minutes with a pressure cooker; 40 minutes with a deep pan; and as indicated in the rice cooker manual

Total time: 30 minutes with a pressure cooker; 55 minutes with a deep pan

**Mutton *Biryani***

*Ingredients*

*For the mutton:*

Mutton pieces -800 grams (28oz) (4 cups)

Chopped Onion-3 large

Chopped Ginger-2 inch piece

Chopped Garlic-8 Cloves

Tomatoes-2

Yoghurt-1 tablespoon

Coriander powder-2 teaspoon

*Garam Masala*-1 teaspoon

Tip: If you can't get ready-made *garam masala* mixture from a nearby Indian store, you can make yours by using 1 black cardamom, 3 green cardamoms, 4 cloves, and 1 inch cinnamon-all ground together for this dish.

Red chilli powder-1/4 teaspoon (enough only to add flavour and not to make it hot)

Cumin seeds-1/2 teaspoon

Cooking Oil-2 tablespoon

*Ghee* (Clarified butter)-2 tablespoon

Water- 1 cup (just to ensure that the mutton cooks and doesn't burn)

Salt to taste

*For the rice:*

Long grain rice (Basmati)-2 cups

Chicken stock-4 cups

Black Cumin seeds (*Shahi Jeera*)-1/2 teaspoon

Green Cardamom (*Chhoti elaichi*)-4

Brown Cardamom (*Badi elaichi*)-2

Cinnamon (*Dalchini*)-1 inch

Cloves (*Laung*)-6

Bay leaf (*Tejpatta*)-1

Clarified butter (*Ghee*)-1 tablespoon

Salt to taste

Sugar-1/2 teaspoon

Few strands of saffron dissolved in ¼ cup milk

Blanched Almonds-24 kernels

*(To blanch almonds, immerse them in half a cup of hot water for 30 minutes. Remove the skin thereafter.)*

*Method*

First of all, wash the rice well (*in a vessel 3-4 times, but don't rub it lest the grains break*) and let it naturally "dry", on an inclined plate, for 15-20 minutes. This helps enhance the aroma.

Next, prepare the chicken stock. Put in a vessel, the neck and wings of the chicken and pour 4 cups of water over it. Now add ½ inch piece of cinnamon, one green cardamom, and two cloves.

If using pressure cooker, cook under full pressure for 5 minutes.

If not using a pressure cooker then let the stock be made for half an hour on low heat.

Remove the chicken pieces, strain and keep the stock ready.

*Now prepare the mutton:*

In a pressure cooker, add the oil and put it on your heat source.

As the oil turns hot, add the cumin seeds and let it splutter.

Immediately add the chopped onion.

Stir well till the onions become translucent.

Now, add the chopped ginger and garlic and stir till it starts giving off a nice aroma.

Add the mutton pieces and the *ghee* (clarified butter).

Stir well.

Add the coriander powder, *garam masala* and red chilli powder.

Stir and cook the mutton pieces till all the water evaporates and the mutton becomes almost dry. This process ensures that all the raw flavours of mutton, onions, etc. are removed.

Now add the tomatoes and the yoghurt.

Stir well again and add the salt.

Let the tomatoes cook well.

Now, add the water, and close the lid of the pressure cooker with weight.

Let it come to full pressure (*i.e. when the weight lifts and there is a whistling sound*).

Turn the heat to low and cook for another 15 minutes.

If not using a pressure cooker, then cook till the mutton becomes tender.

Remove the weight from the cooker and dry the mutton completely in the open cooker itself.

In a wok, add the clarified butter and black cumin seeds, green cardamom, brown cardamom, cinnamon, cloves and bay leaves.

As soon as you start getting a nice aroma, in less than a minute, add the rice along with the salt and sugar.

Do please make sure that the spices brown and not burn, otherwise your dish will be totally spoiled.

Stir well.

Now, add the rice to the cooked mutton in the pressure cooker.

Add the chicken stock and the saffron dissolved in milk and the blanched almonds.

Gently stir so that the mixture is well blended but the rice doesn't break.

Now, close the lid of the pressure cooker without the weight and place on the heat source.

As soon as the steam starts escaping, reduce the heat to low and let it cook for 10 minutes.

Switch off the heat source and let the cooker cool for about 10 minutes before opening its cover.

This helps all the flavours to seep into the rice and the mutton pieces.

That's all. Your delicious mutton *biryani* is ready.

In case not using a pressure cooker, then place the cooked mutton and the prepared rice in a deep thick bottomed vessel along with the chicken stock, saffron and almonds.

Gently stir and then place the vessel on the heat source. As soon as the stock starts boiling, reduce the heat source and close with a tight fitting lid.

The *biryani* should be ready in about 15 minutes but you should check by pressing one grain of rice to see if the rice has been properly cooked.

After switching off the heat source, leave the *biryani* inside the deep pan with the lid tightly shut for another 10 minutes. This helps all the flavours to seep into the rice and the mutton.

You can even decorate your *biryani* with boiled eggs cut in half.

*If using a rice cooker*

Prepare the rice and the mutton as indicated above.

Put the ingredients in the rice cooker and add the chicken stock, saffron and almonds.

Stir gently.

Switch on the rice cooker and the let the rice cook. The rice cooker will switch off on its own when the rice is cooked.

Prep time: 30 minutes

Cooking time: 35 minutes with a pressure cooker; 75 minutes with a deep pan; and as indicated in the rice cooker manual

Total time: 65 minutes with a pressure cooker; 105 minutes with a deep pan

# Chapter 5

## Rice as Snacks and Accompaniments

There is a great tradition of using rice flakes (*chiura* or *poha*), rice puffs (*lai* or *moori*), and ground rice as snacks in India. We present a few samples here.

### *Chiura* or *Poha* Fry (Savoury Rice Flakes)

This is a very popular snack of Maharashtra as well as of Bihar.

*Ingredients*

Rice Flakes (*Chiura/Poha*)-1 cup

Raw peanuts-1/2 cup

Salt and pepper to taste

Oil-1/2 cup

## Method

In a wok or sauce pan, heat the oil and fry the peanuts till golden brown. Take them out in a bowl.

Do not let the peanuts brown too much or the peanuts will start tasting bitter.

Please remember. The peanuts keep cooking in their own heat even when the peanuts are out of the pan.

Now in the same oil, add the rice flakes about a tablespoon at a time. As soon as these puff up, remove to a plate covered with a paper napkin to absorb the excess oil.

Repeat till all the rice flakes are fried.

In a bowl, mix together the peanuts and the rice flakes. Add the salt and pepper while the flakes are still warm otherwise the salt will not stick well to the flakes.

Let this mixture cool down. You can now store it (up to a week) in air tight containers to be used whenever you feel like having a savoury snack.

In addition to (or instead of) peanuts, you can also add cashew nuts/almonds following the same methodology.

In place of any of these nuts, you can also add some fresh peas simply sautéed with butter and cumin seeds. But this will have to be eaten fresh as the peas will not store that well as the nuts mentioned above.

Prep time: 2 minutes

Cooking time: 2 minutes

Total time: 4 minutes

## *Poha* (Cooked Rice Flakes)

This is a very popular snack of Maharashtra as well as of Bihar.

*Ingredients*

Rice Flakes (*Chiura/Poha*)-1 cup

Raw peanuts-1/2 cup

Black Mustard seeds (*Rai*)-1 teaspoon

Curry Leaves-10

Chopped Ginger-1

Boiled Potato-2 (cut into bite size pieces)

Peas-1/2 cup

Salt and pepper to taste

Turmeric (*Haldi*)-1/2 teaspoon

Oil-2 tablespoon

*Method*

Wash the rice flakes and drain all the water. Keep the rice flakes ready along with the boiled and cut potatoes.

In a wok or sauce pan, heat the oil and fry the peanuts till golden brown. Take them out in a bowl.

Do not let the peanuts brown too much or the peanuts will start tasting bitter.

Please remember the peanuts keep cooking in their own heat even when the peanuts are out of the pan.

Now in the same oil, add the black mustard seeds and when they start spluttering add the curry leaves and chopped ginger.

Now add the peas and sauté till the peas are cooked. Add the turmeric and stir well.

Add the rice flakes and the potatoes along with the salt and pepper. Stir well.

Switch off the heat source and add the fried peanuts.

Your delicious *poha* is ready.

Prep time: 7 minutes

Cooking time: 7 minutes

Total time: 14 minutes

## *Idlis* (Steamed rice and lentil cakes)

This is the classic breakfast dish from South India using fermented ground rice, which makes this dish bristling with vitamin B. Lentils add a dash of protein too.

*Ingredients*

*Urad dal* (split black lentils) -1/2 cup

Rice flour-1 cup

*Poha* (rice flakes) - 1 tablespoon

Baking powder-1 level teaspoon

Salt-1/2 teaspoon

Cooking Oil/Clarified butter for greasing the *idli* mould

*Method*

Soak the *urad dal* for at least 4 hours and then make it into a fine paste in a blender.

Add the rice flour, *poha* and some water to make a thick batter and blend again.

Pour this mixture into a vessel and let it ferment (that is let the batter puff up) for the next 12 to 24 hours, depending on what the ambient temperatures are. If it is too cold, then wait for 24 hours and go ahead.

Before steaming the *idlis*, add the salt and baking powder.

Grease the *idli* mould and then pour a tablespoon of the *idli* batter into each.

If using pressure cooker, add water in the cooker which comes below the last mould.

Place the *idli* mould in the cooker.

Close the lid without the weight.

Light the heat source and place your cooker on it.

When steam starts coming out, reduce the heat (to SIM on a gas stove) and cook for about 10-15 minutes or till the *idlis* become firm and can be easily taken out of the mould.

Switch off the heat source.

Remove the *idli* mould from the water and gently nudge out the *idlis* onto a serving plate.

These taste excellent with *sambar* and coconut chutney.

Prep time: Overnight (for soaking, grinding and mixing the *idlis*)

Cooking time: 15 minutes

Total time: Overnight + 15 minutes

## Dosa

This classic breakfast dish from South India has attained the stature of being the most popular street food in India for any time of the day. Use of fermented ground rice makes this dish bristling with vitamin B, while lentils add a dash of protein.

*Ingredients*

*Urad dal* (split black lentils) -1 cup

Rice flour-2 cups

Salt-1/2 teaspoon

Baking Powder- 1 teaspoon

Cooking Oil/Butter-1 tablespoon per *dosa*

*Method*

Soak the *Urad Dal* in two cups of water over night or for at least six hours.

Take out the soaked dal from the water, put it in a blender, and blend well using some water BUT DO NOT LET IT BECOME TOO WATERY.

The batter should feel absolutely smooth to the touch.

In this mixture, add the rice flour and some water and switch on the blender again to turn this all into a thick batter which has a pouring consistency.

Pour the mixture into a suitable vessel, cover it and let it ferment (that is let the batter puff up) for the next 12 to 24 hours, depending on what the ambient temperatures are. If it is too cold, then wait for 24 hours and go ahead.

Add the salt and baking powder, when you are ready to cook.

In a large non-stick girdle, spread about half a cup of batter evenly.

Put it on your heat source.

Let the *dosa* cook.

Add the oil on the top side and a little on the corners.

Do not disturb the *dosa* till it starts browning.

You can then gently nudge the *dosa* at the edge and it will come out on its own when it is done.

Remove the *dosa* to a plate.

It is greater fun if you can eat it right away, with some masala filling and coconut chutney.

Add *sambar* too for a full authentic South Indian experience.

For the next *dosa*, you will need to cool down the girdle OTHERWISE YOU WILL NOT BE ABLE TO SPREAD THE BATTER.

To do so, therefore, wash the girdle in cold water and repeat the above mentioned process till you make the required quantity of *dosas*.

Prep time: Overnight (for soaking, grinding and mixing the *dosas*)

Cooking time: 15 minutes

Total time: Overnight + 15 minutes

## *Baigun Bhaja* (Aubergine fries)

This dish, like the Indian *pakoras,* uses rice flour to impart crispiness. Although the quantity of rice used is very little, we are including this dish here simply because it is a great accompaniment of the Eastern Indian *Khichdi*.

*Ingredients*

Fat round purple Aubergine-1

Turmeric-1 teaspoon

Salt- to taste

Rice flour-1 tablespoon full

Mustard Oil -3 tablespoon

*Method*

Finely slice the aubergine into round pieces.

Sprinkle the salt and turmeric on both sides.

Sprinkle the rice flour and again let it cover all pieces on all sides well.

In a non-stick frying pan, heat the oil and add the aubergine pieces.

Let it brown on one side and then turn it over and brown the other side equally well.

(If you need to handle more aubergines, then fry them batch wise.)

Gently remove from the pan and put it in a dish lined with an absorbent paper napkin. This helps in soaking up the excess oil from the aubergine.

Put these in a serving dish and enjoy your baigun bhaja.

Prep time: 5 minutes

Cooking time: 2 minutes@ each batch of aubergines to be fried

Total time: Approximately 12-15 minutes

# Chapter 6

## Rice as Desserts

Please note that the recipes listed in this chapter cannot be made in a rice cooker.

### *Chawal Ka Kheer* (Rice Pudding)

This is again a North Indian dessert that the gods are very fond of. So don't be surprised to be served this *Kheer* with *Pooris* outside Hindu temples, even outside India.

*Ingredients*

Full cream milk-1 litre (2 US pints liquid) (4 cups)

Rice-2 heaped tablespoon (washed well)

Sugar to taste - (start with 3 tablespoons)

Milk Powder-2 tablespoons

Green Cardomom-2 crushed

Saffron-few strands (optional)

*Method*

In a heavy bottomed wok, bring the milk to boil.

Add the rice which should have been washed well.

Keep stirring on low heat making sure that NOTHING BURNS.

As the mixture begins to thicken, add the milk powder, sugar, the cardamom and the saffron.

Stir well and keep stirring for about 5 minutes.

Switch off the heat source.

That's all.

Your delicious *Kheer* (Rice Pudding) is ready.

You can either have it hot as some like it. Or you could let it cool down, then put it in the fridge and have it chilled.

Prep time: 1 minute

Cooking time: 20 minutes

Total time: 21 minutes

## *Natun Gud Ka Kheer* (Rice Pudding with Palm Jaggery)

This is an out-of-this-world dessert from Eastern India with such subtle flavours that you will just fall in love with.

*Ingredients*

Full cream milk-1 litre (2 US pints liquid) (4 cups)

Rice-2 heaped tablespoon (washed well)

Palm Jaggery (crushed) - 3 tablespoons

Milk Powder-2 tablespoons

*Method*

In a heavy bottomed wok, bring the milk to boil.

Add the rice which should have been washed well.

Keep stirring on low heat making sure that NOTHING BURNS.

As the mixture begins to thicken, add the milk powder.

Stir well and keep stirring for about 5 minutes.

Switch off the heat source and add the palm jaggery.

Stir well.

Note: DON'T add the palm jaggery when the milk is still on the fire as this may curdle the milk.

That's all.

Your *Natun Gud Kheer* is ready.

You can either have it hot as some like it. Or let it cool down, then put it in the fridge and have it chilled.

Prep time: 1 minute

Cooking time: 20 minutes

Total time: 21 minutes

## *Phirni* (Ground Rice Custard)

This used to be a favourite dessert of the Muslim rulers of India.

*Ingredients*

Full cream milk-1 litre (2 US pints liquid) (4 cups)

Rice-2 heaped tablespoon

Sugar to taste - (start with 3 tablespoons)

Milk Powder-2 tablespoons

Green Cardomom-2 crushed

Saffron-few strands dissolved in a tablespoon warm milk

*Method*

Wash the rice well and then let it dry.

Crush the same coarsely.

In a heavy bottomed wok, bring the milk to boil. Add the milk powder.

Add the coarsely ground rice.

Keep stirring on low heat making sure that NOTHING BURNS.

As the mixture begins to thicken, add the sugar, cardamom and the saffron.

Stir well and keep stirring for about 5 minutes or till the whole mixture becomes like a thick custard.

Switch off the heat source and pour the mixture into small individual servings bowl and let it set.

That's all.

Your delicious *Phirni* is ready.

Let it cool down and then put it in the fridge and have it chilled.

Prep time: 10 minutes

Cooking time: 20 minutes

Total time: 30 minutes

## Sweet Rice With Mango

*Ingredients*

Rice-1 cup (washed)

Coconut Milk-1 cup

Water-1 cup

Palm Sugar/Sugar-4 teaspoon

Ripe Mango-1 (cut into bite size pieces)

*Method*

*Method using a pressure cooker*

Place the rice, coconut milk, water and sugar in the cooker and light the heat source.

Close the lid and let the cooker come to full pressure.

Reduce the heat and let the rice cook for 2 more minutes.

Switch off the heat source and let the cooker cool on its own.

Take out the rice in individual serving bowls and decorate it with ripe mangoes.

You can either have it cool or at room temperature.

*Method using a thick bottomed pan*

Place the rice, coconut milk, water and sugar in the pan and light the heat source.

After the water boils, reduce the heat and cover the pan with the lid.

Keep checking occasionally to see if the rice has cooked and all the water and the coconut milk has been absorbed.

Switch off the heat source and let the rice cool on its own.

Take out the rice in individual serving bowls and decorate it with ripe mangoes.

You can either have it cool or at room temperature.

Prep time: 5 minutes

Cooking time: 7 minutes with a pressure cooker; 20 minutes with a pan

Total time: 12 minutes with a pressure cooker; 25 minutes with a pan

**Sweet *Pongal***

*Ingredients*

Rice-3/4 cup

*Moong Dal* (Bengal Gram)-1/4 cup

Jaggery (Gud which is unprocessed sugar)-1 cup

Roasted Cashew nuts-2 tablespoon (fried golden and then chopped up).

*The method to fry the cashew nuts: in a small pan, add about a tablespoon of cooking oil. Put the pan on your heat source. When the oil heats up, add the cashew nuts and stir till they turn golden. Immediately remove the cashew nuts to a plate and chop. Remember if you leave the cashew nuts in the pan, the hot oil will keep roasting the cashew nuts and burn them.*

*Ghee* (clarified butter)-2 tablespoon

Water-3 cups

*Method*

Wash the rice and dal together and let it dry for 5 minutes on an inclined plate.

*If using a pressure cooker:*

In a pressure cooker, put the clarified butter and put it on your heat source.

As it warms up, add the rice and lentils.

Stir well.

Add 2 cups of water and put the lid with the weight on the cooker.

After the cooker comes to full pressure (don't worry, you will hear that typical sound), switch off the heat source but do NOT release the pressure.

Let the pressure cooker cool down by itself.

Meanwhile, in a pan, melt the jaggery with 1 cup water and let it come to a boil.

Open the cooker and add the boiled jaggery to it along with the roasted cashew nuts.

Mix well.

Your Sweet *Pongal* is ready.

*If using a thick bottomed pan/vessel:*

In a pan/vessel, add the clarified butter and place it on your heat source.

When the butter warms up, add the rice and lentil.

Stir well.

Add 2 cups of water.

Cover the pan/vessel with a well-fitting lid.

Reduce the heat to minimum.

In other words, if cooking on gas, turn the knob to SIM (mer). Let the Pongal cook for 15-20 minutes.

Switch off the heat source and let the rice remain in the vessel for another 5 minutes.

Meanwhile, in another pan, melt the jaggery with 1 cup water and let it come to a boil.

Open the vessel and add the boiled jaggery to it along with the roasted cashew nuts.

Mix well.

Your Sweet *Pongal* is ready.

Prep time: 5 minutes

Cooking time: 10 minutes with a pressure cooker; 20-25 minutes with a deep pan

Total time: 15 minutes with a pressure cooker; 25-30 minutes with a deep pan

## *Sakkarai Pongal* (Sweet rice-lentil dessert with milk)

*Ingredients*

Rice-3/4 cup

*Moong Dal* (Bengal Gram)-1/4 cup

Jaggery (Gud which is unprocessed sugar)-1 cup

Roasted Cashew nuts-2 tablespoon (fried golden and then chopped up)

*The method to fry the cashew nuts: in a small pan, add about a tablespoon of cooking oil. Put the pan on your heat source. When the oil heats up, add the cashew nuts and stir till they turn golden. Immediately remove the cashew nuts to a plate and chop. Remember if you leave the cashew nuts in the pan, the hot oil will keep roasting the cashew nuts and burn them.*

Raisins- 2 tablespoon

Green Cardamom (*Chhoti Elaichi*) - 3 crushed

Saffron- 9-10 strands, dissolved in 2 tablespoons of warm milk

*Ghee* (clarified butter)-2 tablespoon

Water-2 cups

Milk- 4 cups

## Method

Wash the rice and dal together and let it dry for 5 minutes on an inclined plate.

*If using a pressure cooker:*

In a pressure cooker, put the clarified butter and put it on your heat source.

As it warms up, add the rice and lentils.

Stir well.

Add 2 cups of water and put the lid with the weight on the cooker.

After the cooker comes to full pressure (*don't worry, you will hear that typical sound*), switch off the heat source but do NOT release the pressure.

Let the pressure cooker cool down by itself.

Open the cooker and add the milk.

Put the cooker on the heat source and let the milk come to a boil.

Add the jaggery and let the mixture thicken.

Keep stirring gently so that the mixture doesn't burn or boil over.

Now add the dissolved saffron and the crushed cardamom.

Stir well. The consistency should now be of a thick custard.

Switch off the heat source.

Keeping aside a few raisins and roasted cashew nuts for decorating the dish, add the remaining raisins and the roasted cashew nuts.

Mix well.

Now decorate the dish with the raisins and roasted cashew nuts that you had kept aside and serve.

Your *Sakkarai Pongal* is ready.

*If using a thick bottomed pan/vessel:*

In a pan/vessel, add the clarified butter and place it on your heat source.

When the butter warms up, add the rice and lentil.

Stir well.

Add 2 cups of water.

Cover the pan/vessel with a well-fitting lid.

Reduce the heat to minimum.

In other words, if cooking on gas, turn the knob to SIM (mer). Let the Pongal cook for 15-20 minutes.

Switch off the heat source and let the rice remain in the vessel for another 5 minutes.

Open the vessel and add the milk.

Put the vessel on the heat source and let the milk come to a boil.

Add the jaggery and let the mixture thicken.

Keep stirring gently so that the mixture doesn't burn or boil over.

Now add the dissolved saffron and the crushed cardamom.

Stir well. The consistency should now be of a thick custard. Switch off the heat source.

Keeping aside a few raisins and roasted cashew nuts for decorating the dish, add the remaining raisins and the roasted cashew nuts.

Mix well.

Now decorate the dish with the raisins and roasted cashew nuts that you had kept aside and serve.

Your *Sakkarai Pongal* is ready.

Prep time: 7 minutes

Cooking time: 20 minutes with a pressure cooker; 30-35 minutes with a deep pan

Total time: 27 minutes with a pressure cooker; 37-42 minutes with a deep pan

## Sweet *Poha Kheer* (Rice Flakes Pudding)

*Ingredients*

Rice Flakes-1 cup

Milk-4 cups

Sugar-8 teaspoons or to taste

*Method*

Wash the rice flakes and drain all the water.

Light the heat source and in a wok or deep pan, bring the milk to boil. To the boiling milk, add the sugar and let it dissolve well.

Now add the rice flakes and again let the mixture come to a boil.

Switch off the heat source.

Your rice flake pudding is ready.

This dish tastes excellent hot especially when you add sliced ripe bananas to the same.

Prep time: 3 minutes

Cooking time: 7 minutes

Total time: 10 minutes

# Appendix

## An Introduction to the Common Indian Spices

It is easy to be overwhelmed with the sheer number and variety of fresh herbs and spices that are commonly used in Indian cuisine. I shouldn't, therefore, make this topic even more complicated by giving the scientific or botanical names of such spices, or where they grow, or how these are harvested and processed. There are many excellent books who have done better justice to this topic.

What I shall attempt here is to just list out some spices that you should experiment with when you are just starting out with "Home Style" Indian cooking.

Here is then my list, in alphabetical order.

***Asafoetida (Hing)***: This is used in small quantities for imparting a strong smell. It is considered very healthy for digestive purposes though some people may find the smell unpleasant and strong. Don't use your saffron with *Hing*, therefore, ever!

**Bay Leaves (Tej Patta):** Used as a flavouring agent.

**Cardamom (Elaichi)**: Please note that the left hand side picture is of brown cardamom and the right hand side picture is of green cardamom.

These come in two varieties: one is small, pale-green and the other is large and brown/black. The pale green variety is used in many Indian dishes including desserts. The brown variety is used for making curries or *pulaos*, but not in sweetmeats.

**Chilli (Kashmiri Red variety)**: In our recipes, we have suggested the use of Kashmiri Red Chillies as these impart a nice red colour and are not as hot as are the other red chillies. In case, you like your food to be really hot, then you can use the other red chillies available in the market which are much hotter.

**Cinnamon (Dalchini)**: This looks like the thin bark of a tree and imparts a lovely flavour both to the sweet and curried dishes. In India, however, it is more used for curries as Indians like Cardamom in their desserts much more than Cinnamon.

**Cloves (Laung):** These look like dried flower buds and add a lovely flavour to the food. Cloves are supposed to have antiseptic qualities which helps preserve food.

***Coconut (Nariyal) powder or milk***: This is used commonly in many South Indian and coastal Indian preparations.

***Coriander seeds and fresh green leaves (Dhania and Dhania patta)***: The dried seeds of Coriander form an essential part of Indian curries and are used quite extensively. The fresh green leaves are used for making Chutneys (Indian sauce) as well as for sprinkling on curries. Since the fresh leaves have a strong flavour, they should only be used by those who really like it.

***Cumin seeds (Jeera)***: Cumin is another essential ingredient of Indian cuisine and is generally the first spice to go into the heated cooking oil before other items are added.

***Curry leaves (Kare-patta)***: These leaves have a lovely flavour and are absolutely essential if you like South Indian cuisine. In India, it grows in abundance and so is easily the cheapest herb to use. Generally used fresh, these can also be dried and used as they retain much of their fragrance even in the dried form.

***Garam Masala***: This is a mixture in equal quantities of cinnamon, cloves, cardamom (both pale-green and brown variety) and whole black pepper corns. These can be ground together and kept in air tight containers for future use for up to a week. Some dishes can also be made by putting the whole spices in oil/ clarified butter (*Ghee*).

All lovers of Indian cooking must learn to use this mixture properly. If you cook Indian dishes only occasionally, you may be tempted to use the commercially available *Garam Masala* powders. Please remember, however, that to economise on costs, some manufacturers skimp on the more expensive ingredients mentioned above and instead add lots of coriander powder, cumin powder, turmeric powder, red chilli powder etc. to add volume. They even add *Kastoori Methi* which just drowns the subtle flavours of other *Garam Masalas*. So do check before you buy such a ready mix of spices.

**Mustard seeds black (*Rai*)**: These are black mustard seeds which look the same as the yellow variety but are supposed to be more pungent than their yellow cousins. This mustard seed is used a lot in South Indian and Western Indian cooking.

**Saffron (*Kesar*)**: Easily the most expensive spice in the world, this comes from the stamen of the saffron flower. It has thread like strands in dark orange colour which when dissolved in milk or water gives out its colour along with its mild, earthy flavour. Not a spice to be used casually, saffron is used mostly in making desserts and some exotic dishes.

**Turmeric (*Haldi*)**: This is easily the commonest and the most important ingredient in any Indian curry dish. Though it does not have much of a flavour, it has a dark yellow colour and a lot of therapeutic value.

***Yoghurt (Dahi)***: Not really a spice or herb, yoghurt is frequently used in many Indian dishes. The variety used in cooking is cultured yoghurt and is always unflavoured. That way it comes closest to the Greek variety of yoghurt.

## A Big Thank You!

Thank you so much for purchasing my book. I know that you could have picked up any other book on this subject but you took a chance with my book.

So a big THANKS for purchasing this book and reading it all the way to the end.

If you liked this book, I shall be grateful if you could do me a small favour.

Please take a moment to leave a review on Amazon, if you are happy.

If not, please tell me directly.

Your feedback is of immense value to me as an Author. Your suggestions will help me in writing the kind of books that you love.

# Excerpt from Home Style Indian Cooking In A Jiffy

## Chapter 4: What Other Strange Things Do You Need To Know About Indian Cuisine?

India is a land of strange sights, sounds, smells, customs, traditions, and of course cuisine. But regardless of where you go in India, you will find some common thread binding its varied culinary traditions together. I underline a few here.

***Eating in Thalis***: Traditionally, Indian food used to be served in *Thalis* (round platters), that is everything, from starters to desserts would be served in one go. That is how it is still done on weddings, or on such special occasions, in many parts of India. The guests usually sit on the floor, cross legged and are served on a banana leaf or on plates made of broad leaves.

Food, if not served in one go in a *Thali*, would be served on your leaf plate in a continuous stream. At the end of it all, the leaf plates along with the food remnants will be fed to the cows, thus earning merit for all concerned. No dishwashing, and the most environmentally benign waste disposal possible, you will have to salute the ancient Indians for thinking of everything!

If you would like to sample a typical North Indian or South Indian *Thali,* do look out for a branch of restaurant chains like Sagar Ratna, Naivedyam, Rajdhani etc. or ask your local hosts for suggestions, when you are next in India.

**No Soup, Dal a distant substitute**: As you'd immediately notice, soups don't precede a normal Indian meal. In a multi-cuisine restaurant, if you insist, you may be offered a Western or Chinese soup. Some try to even take out the curry from any yoghurt based Chicken dish and serve its diluted version as Chicken *Shorba* (soup). The British came up with a lentil based Mulligatawny soup but it still hasn't become mainstream.

India being a tropical country, it was probably not necessary to serve soup in the beginning of a meal to warm you up. It is surprising, however, that even culinary traditions of the colder areas, for example in the Himalayan region of India, too don't serve any soup. Kashmiris and Garhwalis have all kinds of curries but no soup. The nearest thing to soup that the Kashmiris and Ladakhis have is their salted tea, but that they have it all-through-the-day and almost never before a meal!

Indian cuisine also doesn't involve boiling its meats and veggies first and then thinking about what to do with the stock thereof. Stock is part and parcel of the Indian curry. And then you have the formidable variety of *dals* that Indians cook. So who needs soups?

**Carbs are central not meats:** If you see an Indian eating at a *dhaba*, you will immediately notice that rice and breads would be forming more than 60% of that meal. The balance 40% would be distributed over meats, veggies and lentils.

Western cuisine will traditionally reverse this proportion in favour of the meats. One reason could be that Europe's prolonged winters, and consequently shorter cultivating season, meant that they could rely less on grains.

Most of the Indian sub-continent, and even the South-East Asian countries had no such constraints. They could easily have two crops, and sometimes even three. Islands like Bali could sow and reap paddy whenever they wanted. But the moment you go to the colder areas of China or Central Asia, you will find meat gaining the upper hand.

Now that the world economies have integrated so much that you can choose what you can put in your meal platter, what should one do? If you have too much meat, you may exceed your protein requirement and invite problems like high cholesterol, renal stones and even Gout. On the other hand, if you have too much of carbs, you could have more calories than your body needs, suffer from protein shortage, become overweight and could be prone to diabetes.

Why not then balance your carbs with proteins and follow, as Lord Buddha advised some 2600 years back, the MIDDLE PATH?

***Curries are compulsory:*** This is so obvious that you just can't miss it. Anywhere you go and you will find curries dominating the Indian meal platter.

Why is it so? One reason could be the need to have lots of water in a tropical country like India. These curries could meet in a very healthy (you are boiling your water after all, aren't you) and appetising manner. The second reason could be that if you are growing so much rice you would need some curry to "wet" it, to make it less sticky and more palatable.

This could be the reason that you have curries in all rice growing regions of the world, even in Thailand, Laos or Myanmar. On the other hand, the non-rice growing and wheat-eating colder areas of China, Afghanistan and Central Asia rely more on barbeques and didn't have much need for curries.

Sweets and salty dishes can be eaten together: This happens, I suppose, because in the *Thali* style of food service there is no way of stopping what you eat first and then next. Certainly in the perfectly democratic world of the Indian cuisine, when you have access to a bevy of salty, sweet, bitter, sour and hot dishes, you also have the full freedom to decide what you want to eat, with what and when. So you will often see children soothing their taste buds with a spoonful of the sweet dish, whenever they would have had a taste of something bitter or hot. Then you would have the somewhat strange spectacle of Gujaratis eating their desserts first and the main meal later.

In temples, you will often be served *Poori-Kheer* (unleavened Indian fried bread with rice pudding) or *Poori-Halwa* (unleavened Indian fried bread with flour dessert) as *prasadam* (blessings).

Can you think of anyone eating an apple pie with roast chicken (together and not as a separate course) anywhere in the world? I'd certainly love to be educated.

Spices not sprinkled on but cooked with: In Indian cuisine, you don't cook something first and then sprinkle some spices on it to make it somewhat palatable. Spices almost always have to be cooked with the main meal to unleash their full flavours and magic.

**Sauces not prepared separately:** It is again a very common practice in Western cuisine to boil or bake something first and then to pour on it a tomato or cheese based sauce or flambé it with some wine or such other alcoholic beverage.

In India, only restaurants semi cook their meats and vegetables and prepare some sauces separately; both to be mixed the moment someone asks for a tomato or onion or yoghurt based dish. This is because for restaurants, speed is of utmost essence. So they have to keep ingredients ready in a semi-finished condition for a quick conversion in to whatever dishes the customers demand.

However, "Home Style" (or even *dhaba*) Indian food is made in one go with everything cooked together. The only thing to "finish" a curry dish could be the sprinkling of some Coriander (Cilantro) leaves. Similarly, *dals* are tempered later with *Ghee* (clarified butter) and *Jeera* (Cumin seeds) or *Rai* (black mustard seeds).

But these are not exactly sauces that are prepared first and poured on to a cooked dish.

**Taste buds continuously titillated with accompaniments like pickles, chutneys, raita, papad...:** Foreigners are aghast at the sheer number of titbits that literally litter a typical Indian *Thali*. So you will have pickles, made from vegetables, fruits, and even fish. Then you have all kinds of *Papadums*, *Baris* or *Tilauris* made from lentils. Added to these would be the home made sauces called Chutneys and sweet marmalade like preparations made from some fruits called *Murabbas*. And in North India, how can you forget the yoghurt based *Raitas*?

Once a European friend asked me if these accompaniments didn't "confuse" your taste buds unnecessarily.

Well, to be frank, they do. But Indians love that "confusion", because as I've already mentioned, an ideal Indian meal must have a balance of all tastes—sour, salty, bitter, hot and sweet.

And the best way to ensure that is by adding accompaniments which are generally readymade (like jams, marmalades and sauces in the West) and don't have to be cooked at the last moment.

***Less use of ovens or barbeques:*** Except in the Northern Indian states like Punjab, where buried-in-the-earth ovens called Tandoor are very popular, there has hardly been any tradition of baking in the mainstream Indian cuisine. Boiling, frying, steaming-- is all there but whatever little barbequing and baking is done, appears to have come to India from Persia, Turkey or the Central Asian regions from where many Muslim rulers of India had come.

Again, I believe, weather played a part here. Europe and many other colder areas of the world had to keep some kind of fire going in their homes all the while to keep them warm. It was a matter of time, therefore, when someone stumbled upon an appliance that could be attached to the fireplace to cook or rather bake things without much supervision. Even the smoke that resulted from such fireplaces was discovered to have the ability to cure, dry and preserve meats and again mainstream Indian cuisine has no tradition of having such "smoked" meats.

But don't worry. Globalisation has ensured that whatever cakes, pies, breads or pizzas you crave for, you will find it available on the Indian shop shelves today.

***Chopsticks can't work, cutlery is optional:*** Chopsticks don't work with Western cuisine either because for that meats or vegetables have to be cut into chopstick-friendly sizes first. Cutlery too is hardly used when you eat a Burger or a Pizza, especially while walking to your office. But can you avoid cutlery in formal dinners?

Well, in India, even in many 5-star hotels, you have to specifically ask for cutlery in their signature Indian restaurants. In weddings, your *Thali* may contain just one spoon for the dessert, if you are lucky.

Many of my European friends can't imagine how you can pick up rice with your fingers and take it to your mouth without half of it falling on the way. To that, I invite them to come and see how expert South Indians can pick up a curry too from their plates (and not their bowls) with their fingers. It's a sight you must not miss while in India.

Till then, just ask for whatever cutlery you need for your Indian meal. You will at least get a spoon, I promise.

***Vegetarian dishes mimic the non-vegetarian taste:*** This happens all the while in the West with soya sausages mimicking the taste and flavours of pork or chicken sausage, for example.

In India, this mimicking takes place in two ways. First, where the non-vegetarian portions of a dish would just be dropped. For example, the popular mutton *Shami Kebab* would be made exactly with the same ingredients but without the mutton mince. You can't do the same with chicken sausage, after dropping the chicken mince, can you?

In the second, you have totally vegetarian versions which are sometimes more prolific than their non-vegetarian counterparts. For example, the normal non-vegetarian *koftas* would be made either with mutton or chicken mince. But its vegetarian versions, trying to mimic the same texture, flavour and taste, would be made of bottle gourd (*Lauki ke Kofte*), jackfruit (*Kathal ke Kofte*), reduced milk (*Khoya ke Kofte*) or one of the lentils (*Moong dal ke Kofte*).

Anoothi Vishal, a noted food critic, has a "hypothesis that this intriguing strain of cooking originated especially to cater to (such matriarchs) who must have surely been interested enough in the relatively more exotic and intricate non-vegetarian dishes that were being cooked up at home but did not want to give up on their religious/caste injunctions."

Be that as it may, do try these beguiling dishes that try to taste like meat dishes, when you are next in India.

***Cinnamon is not used in desserts but, you guessed it, in curries:*** Do you know that Cinnamon (or the Indian *Dalchini*) is one spice that is used both in Eastern (including Indian) as well as Western cuisines?

Indian cuisine is well known to use a mind-numbing variety of spices (the list is indeed long). I have heard quite a few celebrity chefs boasting how a particular kebab recipe of theirs uses thirty-six (or thirty-nine, I don't remember) spices as ingredients. That would be quite an overkill, in my opinion, and I'd definitely not recommend that any casual dabbler in Indian cuisine experiments with more than ten spices in one dish. But, as I said, that's just my personal opinion.

Coming back to Cinnamon, however, I can bet that this would definitely be in that long list of spices that our celebrity chefs use to create their exotic Indian dishes. I am not sure whether any of their remaining 35 or 38 spices would be so definitely used in Western cuisine. I have always wondered, therefore, as to why Cinnamon is one of the few exceptions.

There is no doubt that Cinnamon does impart a lovely flavour to any dish. Who can resist the aroma of a freshly baked Apple Pie, Pumpkin pie or a Cinnamon roll!

This brings me to the next interesting difference that in the West Cinnamon is used for preparing sweet things like desserts and pies. In India, however, it is more used for savoury things like curries, as Indians prefer Cardamom or Saffron in their desserts more. Cinnamon in fact occupies a pride of place in the preparation of the Indian *garam masala*, a spice mixture that is commonly used in chicken curry, *pulaos, biryanis, vegetable dishes*, or even rajma or kidney beans curry. Kashmiris put Cinnamon powder in their tea which they call "*Kehwa*" that is usually served after dinner. Many claim that adding a teaspoon of Cinnamon and honey in your morning tea would protect you from common cold and stomach worries.

That's actually an excellent suggestion from my personal experience.

You can cook with yoghurt: Eating yoghurt is, of course, no big deal. Flavoured or unflavoured, frozen or thawed, plain or fortified with probiotics, made from full cream or skimmed milk----the variety that industrially manufactured yoghurt today comes in is simply mindboggling.

But cooking with yoghurt? You cook with cheese and wine but yoghurt--the question would certainly stump most aficionados of European or American or even Chinese or Thai schools of cooking.

But talk to anyone from any part of India, and you would instantly get a whole list of regional dishes that use yoghurt in quite a "matter-of-fact" way. This is because before tomatoes were brought to India by the Portuguese sometimes in the 16th century, yoghurt was the main ingredient (apart from tamarind and pomegranate seeds) that could add a little sour taste to Indian dishes.

In Kashmir, savour the *wazwan* (a feast usually served on special occasions like weddings) and you'd find the pride of place accorded to *Gushtabbas* (pounded boneless meat balls cooked in yoghurt) or *Yakhni* or *Dhania Kormas* (both containing mutton pieces, with bones, cooked in yoghurt, with different spices).

In western Indian states of Maharashtra or Gujarat, *Kadhi* (made from yoghurt or butter milk with added potato, onions or vegetable fritters) would be omnipresent in all vegetarian platters. Punjabi vegetarians too like a slightly different version of this *Kadhi* but they actually use copious amounts of yoghurt in their popular drink *Lassi* (basically a yoghurt shake).

The Punjabis (as well as the other North-Indian meat eaters) also like to marinate their chicken and mutton with yoghurt before they put it in their tandoors (earthen ovens) or barbeques, or even curries. Yoghurt in these regions is also supposed to bring in good luck as there is a tradition of NOT leaving your house for any long journey or an examination/interview without having at least a spoonful of yoghurt with sugar.

The East, especially the Bengal region, is famous for cooking their fish in yoghurt. Just check out their dishes of *Dahi-Machhli* (fish cooked in yoghurt and *garam masala*) or *Dahi-sarson* (fish cooked in a yoghurt-mustard sauce). Their yoghurt dessert *Mishti-doi* (literally sweet yoghurt) or *Bhapa-doi* (steamed yoghurt) is simply out-of-this-world.

The southern regions of India are so fond of yoghurt that they usually end their meals, not with a dessert, but with curd-rice. Yoghurt is also a very important ingredient of the south-Indian coconut chutney that goes well with south-Indian snacks like *Idlis*, *Vadas* and *Dosas*.

# Acknowledgement

I dedicate this book to my dearest mom who is the original creator of all these recipes. It is simply amazing how she despite being a working mother (she is actually a very senior Indian Administrative Service officer), finds time to not only cook but also experiment with food.

In her quest for experimenting with cooking, she has had the full support of my father and me. Most fathers generally leave their wives to cook while they watch television or go out to play golf. However, I have often seen my father helping my mother in the kitchen without any hesitation. The overall objective used to be to cook meals from scratch within 30 minutes, and it was amazing how often we succeeded in meeting this target. I, therefore, dedicate this book to my father too, who even now takes time off to "advise" me on what my book should focus on, and sometimes even gives editing suggestions.

## Other Books By The Author

HOME STYLE INDIAN COOKING IN A JIFFY

*Amazon #1 Best Seller in Indian and Professional Cooking*

With an amazing compilation of over 100 delectable Indian dishes, many of which you can't get in any Indian restaurant for love or for money, this is unlike any other Indian Cook book. What this book focuses on is what Indians eat every day in their homes. It then in a step-by-step manner makes this mysterious, never disclosed, "Home Style" Indian cooking accessible to anyone with a rudimentary knowledge of cooking and a stomach for adventure.

Prasenjeet Kumar, the corporate lawyer turned gourmand, in this second book of his series "How to Cook everything in a Jiffy" explores the contours of what sets Indian "Home Style" food so apart from restaurant food. In his uniquely semi-autobiographical style, he starts with his quest for Indian food in London, wonders why his European friends don't have such a "strange" debate between "Home Style" and "Restaurant" food, and learns that the whole style of restaurant cooking in India is diametrically opposed to what is practiced in Indian homes with respect to the same dish.

**You may like this book if:**

You are an Indian pining for a taste of your home food anywhere in the world, including India.

You are an Indian, reasonably adept in your own regional cuisine, for example, South Indian cuisine, but want to learn about the "Home Style" culinary traditions of the Eastern and Northern India as well.

You are NOT an Indian but you love Indian cuisine and have wondered if someone could guide you through the maze of spices that Indians use, and help you tame down the oil and chilli levels of many of their dishes.

*Recommends Amazon.com Top 100 Reviewer Mysterious Reviewer "There's plenty to like concerning the Home Style Indian Cooking In a Jiffy cookbook by author Prasenjeet Kumar. Kumar has formatted the book so each recipe links back to the interactive table of contents making navigation easy. He's also included color photos illustrating his recipe throughout his cookbook. Best of all Kumar offers information how to set up a basic kitchen, a brief introduction to Indian spices and goes onto offer various chapters covering Indian food.*

*His recipes offer both the standard cooking method or the option to use a pressure cooker (when appropriate) to prepare the recipe. He gives clear directions how to complete the task using either cooking method..."*

HOW TO CREATE A COMPLETE MEAL IN A JIFFY

*Presenting a Cookbook Like No Other Cookbook in the World*

From the popular website www.cookinginajiffy.com and the author of four Amazon Bestseller cookbooks comes a cookbook that doesn't focus on recipes.

Instead, it shares the secret of creating a Full Meal in around 30 minutes.

How is that possible?

With just Proper Sequencing and Parallel Processing of your actions, is author Prasenjeet Kumar's answer.

So if till now you didn't know (or hadn't thought about) as to how with proper sequencing and parallel processing you can reduce your drudgery by many, many fold, you have come absolutely to the right place.

In that background, the Book presents around 40 dishes grouped into 10 Full Meals consisting of: two "concepts" of breakfasts, four Indian meals, one Thai meal, one Japanese meal, and two Western meals.

# HOW TO COOK IN A JIFFY EVEN IF YOU HAVE NEVER BOILED AN EGG BEFORE

*Introducing "How To Cook In A Jiffy"— The Easiest Cookbook On Earth From The Author Of The Hugely Popular Website www.cookinginajiffy.com*

Never boiled an egg before but want to learn the magic art of cooking? Then don't leave home without this Survival Cookbook. Be it healthy college cooking, or cooking for a single person or even outdoor cooking---this easiest cookbook on earth teaches you to survive all situations with ease.

Where this book scores over other "How To" cookbooks is the structured manner in which it follows a step by step "graduation" process.

Most uniquely, the book teaches the concept of "sequencing and parallel processing" in cooking to enable busy people to create a 3-4 course meal in less than 30 minutes.

The book is fun and entertaining to read with the author sharing his own personal story of bumbling about in the wonderlands of cooking, with wit and humour.

*Recommends Amazon.com reviewer B. Farrell "This is a good informative book for someone starting out in the adventure of cooking. This would make a great gift for a young bride just starting out with her new duties of cooking or a single person getting out on their own."*

# HEALTHY COOKING IN A JIFFY: THE COMPLETE NO FAD NO DIET HANDBOOK

*Amazon #1 in Hot New Releases in Health, Fitness & Dieting> Special Diets> Healthy*

*Amazon #3 Best Seller in Health, Fitness & Dieting> Special Diets> Healthy*

If you have ever wondered how you can be healthy without dieting, following any peculiar fads, eating any esoteric foods, injecting any hormones or downing any pills, potions or supplements, you have come absolutely to the right place.

In fact, without bothering about the risk of sounding so old fashioned, author Prasenjeet Kumar (of the celebrated website cookinginajiffy.com and the writer of the "How to Cook Everything in a Jiffy" series of cookbooks) declares that he does not think that anyone should be on a perpetual diet to stay healthy. In this book, therefore, he recommends that you do not follow any of the rather peculiar diet regimes such as a low carb high protein diet, low fat diet, Vegan diet (unless you truly believe in the vegan philosophy) or any kind of crash diets. From his own experience, he says that that they will all do you more harm than good.

Instead, the author recommends going to the basics that of following a balanced diet regime. In that background, the book presents a veritable cornucopia of easy recipes to give you an idea of what you can cook to achieve your target of having regularly a balanced diet. You will find ideas on how to cook your vegetables in a simple and tasty manner, how to handle pasta recipes, chicken recipes, fish recipes, mutton recipes, milk shakes (even if you hate drinking plain milk), breakfast recipes, lunch and dinner recipes and some Asian recipes when you feel the need to have something different and exciting.

Surprisingly, you will find some supposedly "unhealthy" recipes as waffles, pancakes, French toasts, lasagne and lamb moussaka too in this "healthy" cookbook. The author's short answer is, that the wonderful taste of these dishes makes you happy and being happy (and full of serotonin) is more than half way to being healthy. Moreover, as the author believes, any sensible person will have these dishes only once-in-a-while when you are bored eating your regular stuff.

Again, quite boldly, the author declares that personally he does not count calories in his diet, oops recipes. He feels that counting calories can actually drive you mad. This book celebrates exactly this very viewpoint and deliberately with some justifiable pride eschews providing any calorific or nutritional information for the listed recipes. If you want to still count calories, feel free to do so by taking advantage of so many tools that are readily available on the internet, the author advises.

At the end of this book, there are tips relating to how you can manage to have five to six small meals a day, regardless of your busy schedule, how you can exercise even if you are not a "gym person", how to freeze and preserve leftovers and finally how to sequence and parallel process your actions so that you save time while cooking your meals.

So if you are sick of dieting, counting calories, or gorging on supplements, do consider investing in this book of simply sensible cooking and get on to a journey of eternal joy and happiness.

THE ULTIMATE GUIDE TO COOKING LENTILS THE INDIAN WAY

*Presenting 58 Tastiest Ways to Cook Lentils as Soups, Curries, Snacks, Full Meals and hold your breath, Desserts! As only Indians can.*

From the author of # 1 Amazon Best seller "Home Style Indian Cooking In A Jiffy"

This is simply the ultimate vegetarian protein cookbook.

We all know that as the cheapest and most versatile sources of protein available to mankind, lentils have been cultivated and consumed from the time immemorial.

Lentils are mentioned in religious books such as the Bible, Quran and the Vedas.

Lentils were so important for those long sea voyages that the Romans named their emperors after the most common legumes: Lentulus (lentil), Fabius (fava), Piso (pea), and Cicero (chickpea).

And yet, lentils came to be almost forgotten in the modern post-20th century world with easy availability of red meat and the rise of fast food joints.

Now thanks to scientists and expert bodies like the Mayo Clinic, we know that lentils are actually better than meat.

*Lentils are actually the "Healthiest Food" in the World.*

*Lentils are good for a Healthy Heart*: Lentils contain significant amount of folate and magnesium, both doing wonders for your heart.

*Lentils replenish Iron Needed for Energy*: Lentils are rich in Iron, which is a vital component of energy production and metabolism in the body.

*Lentils are low in cholesterol*: Lentils, unlike red meat, are low in fat, calories and cholesterol. They are also somewhat lower in oxalic acid and similar chemicals which cause stone formation in kidneys and result in gout, a painful affliction of joints caused by the deposition of crystals.

*Lentils are rich in fibre*: If you are looking for ways to reduce constipation, try Lentils as they contain a high amount of dietary fibre, both soluble and insoluble.

The way Indians cook lentils is unmatched by any other cuisine on Planet Earth.

No one can cook lentils the way Indians do.

This is because almost every Indian meal has to have a lentil dish, as dal (soup), curry, snack or dessert. So they have centuries of expertise in turning lentils in whichever way you want.

On the other hand, most western cook books would, at the most, recommend baking lentils with cheese, putting them in hamburgers, having them with sausages and casseroles or making lentils stew.

One is, of course, not counting the lentils sprouts salad or the famous students' dorm dish of baked beans (straight from the can) as well as the West Asian "sauce" hummus, without which no Lebanese meal can be termed complete.

There is nothing wrong if you want to have your lentils this way.

But if you want to experiment, and wish to embark upon a roller coaster culinary adventure, you must look at Indian cuisine.

*"The Ultimate Guide to Cooking Lentils the Indian Way"* lets you savour, in this background, as many as twenty most popular "Home Style" dal recipes; ten curries; six lentil dishes cooked with rice; eleven snacks; three kebabs; three lentil stuffed *parathas*; and five desserts.

It is said that without carrying *Sattu* or roasted chickpea flour with them, for sustenance on those long and arduous treks, Buddhist monks from Bihar could NOT have spread Buddhism to far off places from Afghanistan and Tibet to Korea!

Still don't believe about India's robust lentil tradition?

## Books by the Author in Other Genres

CELEBRATING QUIET PEOPLE: UPLIFTING STORIES FOR INTROVERTS AND HIGHLY SENSITIVE PERSONS

*A unique collection of motivational, inspirational and uplifting TRUE stories for introverts and highly sensitive persons that you shouldn't miss....*

These stories tell us about how really famous introverts such as Abraham Lincoln, Albert Einstein, J.K. Rowling and Walt Disney overcame, with steely resolve, the most difficult challenges thrown their way.

Above all, they highlight the importance of hard work, persistence, self-discipline, and having a vision or a rich imagination which all Quiet persons are fortunately, naturally endowed with.

The author sincerely hopes that these stories will give you the courage to pursue your dreams and ambitions, regardless of how "outlandish" they may seem to others.

QUIET PHOENIX: AN INTROVERT'S GUIDE TO RISING IN CAREER & LIFE

*Amazon #1 Best Seller in Legal Profession and Ethics & Professional Responsibility*

Awaken the Phoenix Bird inside You.

Rise in Your Career. Love Your Profession.

In a first-of-its-kind tell-all memoir on the inside working of a top Indian law firm, corporate lawyer turned author Prasenjeet Kumar, shares his experiences in as candid and no-holds-barred manner as never disclosed in this genre before.

*This makes "Quiet Phoenix" an invaluable, 242 pages, book:*

First, for all law students who have starry eyed notions of working in a corporate law firm;

Second, for those Junior Associates who have just entered the portals of their dream firm and are bewildered, for example, at the senselessly long hours they are required to clock in; and

Third, for the Managing Partners who need to see in the mirror how horrible they look and what they need to do to become human again.

*With extensive research and penetrating insight, the book also focuses on the "problems" of introverts who feel that:*

Their extroverted colleagues are better at marketing themselves and in getting ahead in career;

They feel sick and tired of long working hours;

They don't know how to deal with office bullies;

They are aghast at Co-workers stealing their ideas;

They can't believe that their bosses can practice blatant favouritism;

Or that they can have a Colleague just round the corner who is willing to back stab them without any provocation.

Using everyday office incidents, experiences and politics that anyone (and not just lawyers) can immediately relate to, "Quiet Phoenix" not only inspires but makes you come with your own uniquely actionable plan.

*The characters used in the book are so life-like that they will immediately remind you of someone in your office.*

You have the Senior Associate one Mr. Late Nightaholic who loves to let his juniors twiddle their thumbs the whole day and then at 06.30 pm dumps a lot of work to keep them busy the whole night.

Then you have Ms. Senior Partner, who despite being a junior associate acts as she is the senior partner for all junior associates.

Next is Ms. Goof-up Queen, who is trying to be a senior associate by proving that she is the only one NOT goofing up while everyone around her is churning out sheer garbage.

And at the very top is the partner Mr. Blood Sucker who is where he is because he is a childhood chum of the owner of the firm.

Like the legendary Phoenix bird rising from the ashes "Quiet Phoenix" is meant to specifically help all introverts or Quiet persons to lift them up literally from the bootstraps, by constantly reminding them that introversion is NOT a handicap to be ashamed of. In fact, Introverts are supposed to have amazing powers of concentration, engaged listening, and an ability to foster deep relationships with friends and clients.

Over all, "Quiet Phoenix" is an incredible story that Prasenjeet Kumar shares, with wit and charm, of the journey from being a Corporate Lawyer to becoming a Full Time Author-Entrepreneur using his introversion as strength to overcome all obstacles.

# QUIET PHOENIX 2: FROM FAILURE TO FULFILMENT: A MEMOIR OF AN INTROVERTED CHILD

*Amazon #1 Hot New Releases in Biographies & Memoirs > Professional and Academics > Educators*

Celebrating The Quiet Child: A Must Read For every Parent, Teacher, Mentor, Sports Coach........

From Prasenjeet Kumar, the author of Quiet Phoenix, the Amazon #1 Bestseller in the Hot New Releases category, comes a sequel that no one who deals with introverted children should miss.

The underlying theme of the book is that just as a Phoenix Bird is hardwired to be reborn from the ashes of her ancestors, her tears are meant to cure wounds and she symbolises undying hope and optimism, so is your Quiet child built for persistence, creativity, and self-discipline; and for displaying a knack for self-learning, high emotional intelligence and an impeccable sense of moral responsibility.

*Instead of cherishing such rare traits*

Introverts are sadly often misunderstood by almost every one.

Parents worry if their children prefer spending time in solitude, probably day dreaming.

Teachers presume that if a child hesitates to answer questions, she must be having some kind of learning or even social disability.

Quiet Children have difficulties in making friends, with their classmates seeing them as "weird", "rude" or "arrogant".

They are seen as "over" sensitive to mean comments or bullying.

They appear to lack aggression or as some say 'the will to fight back'.

Overall, introverted children seem to be more flustered about almost every facet of life in noisy and large Public Schools.

*Any advice that Quiet children should be more 'outgoing', 'sociable' and 'active' seems to be counterproductive.*

Any aggressive follow up on this advice often results in your Quiet child losing her self-esteem, forcing her to become even more withdrawn.

*With fables, stories and real incidents from the author's own childhood "Quiet Phoenix 2: From Failure to Fulfilment" reiterates that introvert Children being asked to behave in a more extroverted fashion is like asking a young Phoenix bird to behave like an Eagle.*

Every child is born with some unique traits. The challenge is: how parents, teachers and friends can recognize, nurture and enhance those powers so that every child, quiet or loquacious, becomes a winner.

"Quiet Phoenix 2: From Failure to Fulfilment" sincerely intends to help everyone dealing with 'Quiet Children' to cherish and celebrate them for what they are.

And to help them rise above everything; to lead them towards a path of happiness leaving behind all old memories of pain and isolation; and to turn them into life's winners.

Just like the Phoenix rising from the ashes.

With real life characters like Ms. Brownie Points, Mr. Noisy Ferrari and Ms. Pencil Snatcher, this book is intended for everyone--a parent, teacher, or sports Coach.

Who wants to understand how to harness the powers of Quiet children in an extroverted world.

And if you are an introvert adult, you may find this book useful in understanding yourself, your past and what you want out of life in the future.

So what are you waiting for?

## Connect With The Author

Feel free to write to me anytime at ciaj@cookinginajiffy.com.

I would love to connect with you on Social Media. Join me on:

### Facebook

https://www.facebook.com/cookinginajiffy

### Twitter

https://twitter.com/CookinginaJiffy

### Goodreads

https://www.goodreads.com/prasenjeet

### Google Plus

https://www.google.com/+PrasenjeetKumarAuthor

## About The Author

Prasenjeet Kumar is a Law graduate from the University College London (2005-2008), London University and a Philosophy Honours graduate from St. Stephen's College (2002-2005), Delhi University. In addition, he holds a Legal Practice Course (LPC) Diploma from College of Law, Bloomsbury, London.

Prasenjeet loves gourmet food, music, films, golf and traveling. He has already covered seventeen countries including Canada, China, Denmark, Dubai, Germany, Hong Kong, Indonesia, Macau, Malaysia, Sharjah, Sweden, Switzerland, Thailand, Turkey, UK, Uzbekistan, and the USA.

Prasenjeet is the self-taught designer, writer, editor and proud owner of the website cookinginajiffy.com which he has dedicated to his mother. He is also running another website publishwithprasen.com where he shares tips about writing and self-publishing.

# Index

Aubergine fries, 129
*Baigun Bhaja*, 129
*Bisi Belle Bhath*, 58
*Chana Dal Khichdi*, 48
*Chawal Ka Kheer*, 131
Chicken *Biryani*, 92
Chicken *Kofta Biryani*, 105
*Chiura*, 119
Cooked Rice Flakes, 122
Cumin Rice, 34
Curd Rice, 24
*Dosa*, 126

Dry Fruits *Pulao*, 68
Ground Rice Custard, 135
Hyderabadi Chicken *Biryani*, 101
*Idlis*, 124
*Jeera Pulao*, 34
*Khichdi*, 43
Lemon rice, 26
Light *Khichdi*, 52
*Mattar Pulao*, 63
Mixed Vegetable Cheese *Biryani*, 73
Mutton *Biryani*, 111

*Natun Gud Ka Kheer*, 133
*Navratna Pulao*, 79
Nine Jewels Rice dish, 79
Onion Rice, 32
Peas Rice, 63
*Phirni*, 135
*Poha*, 122
*Poha* Fry, 119
*Pongal*, 55
Prawn Stir Fried Rice, 89
Rice Boiled, 20
Rice Flakes Pudding, 146
Rice Pudding, 131
Rice Pudding with Palm Jaggery, 133
Saffron *pulao*, 38
Saffron rice dish, 38
*Sakkarai Pongal*, 142
Savoury Rice Flakes, 119
Steamed rice cakes, 124
Stir Fried Rice, 85
Sweet *Poha Kheer*, 146
Sweet *Pongal*, 139
Sweet Rice With Mango, 137
Tamarind rice, 28
Tomato rice, 30

Printed in Great Britain
by Amazon